An honest road in life?
contains this descretion

what goes on between you and
your "higher power" you choose
to call God...is better hidden
than secret...

John Paul II's
Book of
Mary

JOHN PAUL II's BOOK OF *Mary*

COMPILED BY

MARGARET R. BUNSON

Our Sunday Visitor Publishing Division
Our Sunday Visitor, Inc.
Huntington, Indiana 46750

Although the materials in this work are from various sources, some minor changes have been made for stylistic consistency only. Nothing has been altered so as to change the meaning of the original. If any copyrighted materials have been inadvertently used in this work without proper credit being given in one form or another, please notify Our Sunday Visitor in writing so that future printings of this work may be corrected accordingly.

ISBN: 0-87973-578-3
LCCCN: 95-73143

Cover design by Monica Watts

PRINTED IN THE UNITED STATES OF AMERICA

578

This book is dedicated to
Sue and John Mikulka of Laurel, Maryland

Acknowledgments

There are a number of individuals to whom a special debt of gratitude is owed for their assistance in the preparation and publication of this volume. Chief among them are: Our Sunday Visitor's Robert Lockwood, President and Publisher; Greg Erlandson, Editor in Chief; Jackie Lindsey, Acquisitions Editor; and Henry O'Brien, Managing Editor of Religious Books.

Table of Contents

Foreword

The Holy Father, Pope John Paul II, has been unwavering in his devotion to Mary, a trusting veneration born out of the perils and triumphs of his personal life. This collection of papal admonitions and meditations has been grouped according to the traditional titles bestowed upon the Mother of the Redeemer, some of which date to the early Church and reflect the vivid languages of the time.

Star of the Sea, for example, is the title used to honor Mary as the guide of pilgrims. Mystical Rose is taken from the description of Mary as the rose blooming in Jesse's branch (denoting Christ's early lineage in the House of David). The ancients used the word "pillar" instead of model, hence her title Pillar of Faith. She is the Gate of Heaven, having brought Christ into the world, as the handmaid of the Lord. She is also the Mirror of Perfection, inspiring Pope John Paul II and this new generation. May we be given the graces of discernment needed in the modern world from Mary, the Seat of Wisdom.

O Most Blessed Virgin Mary,
Mother of Christ and Mother of the Church,
With joy and wonder we seek to make our
    own your *Magnificat,*

joining you in your hymn of thankfulness
and love.
With you we give thanks to God,
"whose mercy
is from generation to generation,"
for the exalted vocation
and the many forms of mission
entrusted to the lay faithful.
God has called each of them by name
to live his own communion of love
and holiness
and to be one
in the great family of God's children.
He has sent them forth
to shine with the light of Christ
and to communicate the fire of the Spirit
in every part of society
through their life
inspired by the Gospel.
O Virgin of the *Magnificat*,
fill their hearts
with gratitude and enthusiasm
for this vocation and mission.
With humility and magnanimity
you were the "handmaid of the Lord";
give us your unreserved willingness
for service to God
and the salvation of the world.
Open our hearts
to the great anticipation
of the kingdom of God

and of the proclamation of the Gospel
to the whole of creation.
Your mother's heart
is ever mindful of the many dangers
and evils which threaten
to overpower men and women
in our time.
At the same time your heart also takes
notice
of the many initiatives
undertaken for good,
the great yearning for values,
and the progress achieved
in bringing forth
the abundant fruits of salvation.
O Virgin full of courage,
may your spiritual strength
and trust in God inspire us,
so that we might know
how to overcome all the obstacles
that we encounter
in accomplishing our mission.
Teach us to treat the affairs
of the world
with a real sense of Christian responsibility
and a joyful hope
of the coming of God's kingdom, and
of a "new heaven and a new earth."
You who were gathered in prayer
with the Apostles in the Cenacle,
awaiting the coming

of the Spirit at Pentecost,
implore his renewed outpouring
on all the faithful, men and women alike,
so that they might more fully respond
to their vocation and mission,
as branches engrafted to the true vine,
called to bear much fruit
for the life of the world.
O Virgin Mother,
guide and sustain us
so that we might always live
as true sons and daughters
of the Church of your Son.
Enable us to do our part
in helping to establish on earth
the civilization of truth and love,
as God wills it,
for his glory.
Amen.

Christifideles Laici, **December 30, 1988**

1 / Gate of Heaven

Before blessing you, I invite you to pray together. We are going to turn to Mary, our Mother. I am sure that the children here present pray to her often. And you parents, you set great store by training them, from the earliest age, to prayer, to religious acts, to the Good News of the Gospel. Even better, you deepen your faith with them and pray with them. Let us ask Mary to lead you to full knowledge of her Son, Jesus, to be his disciples and his apostles.

Hail, Mary, full of grace, the Lord is with you; blessed are you among women, and blessed is the fruit of your womb, Jesus. Holy Mary, Mother of God, pray for us sinners, now, and at the hour of our death. Amen!

Address, Rome, November 10, 1980

. . . [T]he Second Vatican Council emphasizes in the last chapter of the *Dogmatic Constitution on the Church* that "in her life the Virgin has been a model of motherly love with which all who join in the Church's apostolic mission for the regeneration of mankind should be animated" (*Lumen Gentium*, 65).

Audience, Rome, November 28, 1980

What can I wish for you but that you will always listen to these words of Mary, the Mother of Christ: "Do whatever he tells you"? And may you accept these words with your hearts, because they were uttered from the heart. From the heart of Mother. And that you will fulfill them: "God has chosen you . . . calling you to this, with our Gospel, for possession of the glory of our Lord, Jesus Christ."

Insegnamenti, January 20, 1980

In this international Year of the Family, we place our hope in the Blessed Virgin Mary, first of the disciples and Mother of all disciples, model of strength and perseverance in following Christ to the cross. The Virgin Mary is the prototype of consecrated life because she is the Mother who welcomes, listens to, beseeches, and contemplates her Lord in heartfelt praise. We pray to her for all consecrated men and women so that she, as our Mother, may protect, comfort, and renew all the families of consecrated life in the Church.

Address, Rome, October 27, 1994

Above all, I implore Mary, the heavenly Mother of the Church, to be so good as to devote herself to this prayer of humanity's new advent, together with us who make up the Church, that is to say, the Mystical Body of her only Son. I hope that through this prayer we will be able to receive the Holy Spirit coming upon us and thus become Christ's witnesses "to the ends of the earth," like those who went out from the Upper Room of Jerusalem on the day of Pentecost.

Redemptor Hominis, 22

As Paul the Apostle says: "We know that our home is in heaven, where we also await our Lord Jesus Christ, the Savior, who will change our vile body that it may be fashioned like his magnificent body" (Phil. 3:20-21). Holy Mary has already reached her heavenly home, and after exile on earth gained entrance immediately to glory. So, let your sufferings, your anxieties, your hopes be directed toward her, that her help in joining her after this exile on earth will not fail.

With this wish I bless you all from the bottom of my heart.

Address, Rome, August 13, 1980

The Letter to the Ephesians, speaking of the "glory of grace" that "God the Father has bestowed on us in his beloved Son," adds: "In him we have redemption through his blood" (Eph. 1:6-7). According to the belief formulated in the solemn documents of the Church, this "glory of grace" is manifested in the Mother of God through the fact that she has been "redeemed in a more sublime manner." By virtue of the richness of the grace of the beloved Son, by reason of the redemptive merits of him who willed to become her Son, Mary was *preserved from the inheritance of original sin.* In this way, from the moment of her conception — which is to say her existence — she belonged to Christ, sharing the salvific and sanctifying grace and in that love which has its beginning in the "Beloved," the Son of the eternal Father, who through the Incarnation became her own Son. Consequently, through the power of the Holy Spirit, in the order of grace, which is participation in the divine nature, Mary receives life from him to whom she herself, in the order of earthly generation, gave life as a mother. The liturgy does not hesitate to call her "Mother of the Creator" and to hail her with words which Dante Alighieri places on the lips of St. Bernard: "daughter of your Son." And since Mary receives this "new life" with a fullness corresponding to the Son's love for the Mother and thus corresponding to the dignity of divine motherhood, the angel of the Annunciation calls her "full of grace."

Redemptoris Mater, 10

Dear brothers and sisters, representatives of the millions of faithful and dedicated Catholic laity of the United States: in bringing my reflections to a conclusion I cannot fail to mention the Blessed Virgin Mary who reveals the Church's mission in an unparalleled manner. She, more than any creature, shows us that the *perfection of love* is the only goal that matters, that it alone is the measure of holiness and the way to perfect communion with the Father, the Son, and Holy Spirit. Her state in life was that of a laywoman, and she is at the same time the Mother of God, the Mother of the Church, and our Mother in the order of grace.

The Council concluded the *Dogmatic Constitution on the Church* with an exhortation on the Blessed Virgin. In doing so, the Council expressed the Church's ancient sentiments of love and devotion to Mary. Let us, especially during this Marian Year, make our own these sentiments imploring her to intercede for us with her Son, for the glory of the Holy and Undivided Trinity (cf. *Lumen Gentium*, 69).

Address, San Francisco, September 18, 1987

Mary shares our human condition, but in complete openness to the grace of God. Not having known sin, she is able to have compassion for every kind of weakness. She understands sinful man and loves with a mother's love. Precisely for this reason she is on the side of truth and shares the Church's burden of recalling always and to everyone the demands of morality. Nor does she permit sinful man to be deceived by those who claim to love him by justifying his sin, for she knows that the sacrifice of Christ her Son would thus be emptied of its power. No absolution offered by beguiling doctrines, even in the areas of philosophy and theology, can make man truly happy. Only the cross and glory of the risen Christ can grant peace to his conscience and salvation to his life.

Veritatis Splendor, **120**

When at the moment of the Annunciation Mary utters her *"fiat"*: "Let it be done to me according to your word," she conceives in a virginal way a man, the Son of Man, *who is the Son of God.* By means of this "humanization" of the Word-Son the self-communication of God reaches its definitive fullness in the history of creation and salvation. This fullness acquires a special wealth and expression in the text of John's Gospel: "The Word became flesh." The Incarnation of God the Son signifies the taking up into unity with God not only of human nature, but *in this human nature, in a sense, of everything that is "flesh":* the whole of humanity, the entire visible and material world. The Incarnation, then, also has cosmic significance, a cosmic dimension. The "firstborn of all creation," becoming incarnate in the individual humanity of Christ, unites himself in some way with the entire reality of man, which is also "flesh" — and in this reality with all "flesh," with the whole of creation.

Dominum et Vivificantem, 50

Beloved, look at the ideal represented by the figure of the Good Shepherd — an ideal of light, life, and love — and, at the same time, consider that our time needs to refer to such ideals. If Christ's eye dwells on you with predilection, if he chooses you, if he calls you to be his collaborators, do not hesitate for a moment — following the example of the most

holy Virgin to the angel — to say your
generous "Yes." You will not regret it; your joy
will be true and full, and your life will appear
rich in fruits and in merits, because you will
become with him and for him messengers of
peace, agents of good, collaborators with God
in the salvation of the world!

Address, Rome, May 6, 1979

Yes, truly "blessed is she who believed!" These
words spoken by Elizabeth after the
Annunciation, here at the foot of the cross,
seem to reecho with supreme eloquence, and
the power contained within them becomes
something penetrating. From the cross, that is
to say, from the very heart of the mystery of
Redemption, there radiates and spreads out
the prospect of that blessing of faith. It goes
back to "the beginning," and as a sharing in
the sacrifice of Christ — the new Adam — it
becomes in a certain sense *the counterpoise to
the disobedience and disbelief* embodied in the
sin of our first parents. Thus teach the Fathers
of the Church and especially St. Irenaeus,
quoted by the Constitution *Lumen Gentium:*
"The knot of Eve's disobedience was untied by
Mary's obedience; what the virgin Eve bound
through her disbelief, the Virgin Mary *loosened
by her faith.*" In the light of this comparison
with Eve, the Fathers of the Church — as the

Council also says — call Mary the "mother of the living" and often speak of "death through Eve, life through Mary."

Redemptoris Mater, 19

Under the protection of the Blessed Virgin Mary, in our common responsibility, for the glory of Christ's name, proclaiming the Good News of salvation — the "Good News of a great joy which will come to all people" (Lk. 2:10). And to all your clergy, religious, and laity I send my apostolic blessing, in the love of Jesus Christ, the Son of God and the Savior of the world.

Address, Rome, October 23, 1980

Moreover, the effectiveness of our pastoral mission depends on our holiness of life. Let us not be afraid, for the Mother of Jesus is with us. She is in our midst today and always. And we are strong through her prayers and safe in her care. *Regina Caeli, laetare, alleluia!*

Address, Kumasi, Ghana, May 9, 1980

Mary is the first to share in this new revelation of God and, within the same, in this new "self-giving of God." Therefore she proclaims: "For he who is mighty has done great things for me, and holy is his name." Her words reflect a joy of spirit which is difficult to express: "My spirit rejoices in God my Savior." Indeed, "the deepest truth about God and the salvation of man is made clear to us in Christ, who is at the same time the mediator and the fullness of all revelation." In her exultation Mary confesses that she finds herself *in the very heart of this fullness* of Christ. She is conscious that the promise made to the fathers, first of all "to Abraham and to his posterity forever," is being fulfilled in herself. She is aware that concentrated within herself as the Mother of Christ *is the whole salvific economy*, in which "from age to age" is manifested he, who as the God of the Covenant, "remembers his mercy."

Redemptoris Mater, 36

Now, dear brothers: how near you are to the cause of God! How deeply it is imprinted upon your vocation, ministry, and mission. In consequence, in the midst of the People of God that looks to Mary with immense love and hope, you must look to her with exceptional hope and love. Indeed, you must proclaim Christ who is her Son; and who will better communicate to you the truth about him than his Mother? You must nourish human hearts with Christ; and who can make you more aware of what you are doing than she who nourished him? "Hail, true Body born of the Virgin Mary!" In our ministerial priesthood there is *the wonderful and penetrating dimension of nearness to the Mother of Christ.* So let us try to live in that dimension. If I may be permitted to speak here about my own experience, I will say to you that in writing to you I am referring especially to my own personal experience.

"To All Priests of the Church," 11

2 / *Handmaid of the Lord*

"Behold, I am the handmaid of the Lord; let it be done to me according to your word" (Lk. 1:38).

May these words that Mary is pronouncing by the lips of so many human beings be a light on your path for all of you.

Address, Lourdes, May 22, 1979

. . . [I]ndeed, Mary, you are blessed more than all other women.

To her first beatitude Elizabeth adds a second one: "Blessed is she who believed that the promise made her by God will be fulfilled" (Lk. 1:45). Elizabeth extols and praises the faith of Mary. With this she enters in a profound way into the unique greatness of the moment when the Virgin from Nazareth had heard the words of the Annunciation. For this message had burst open all limits in human understanding in spite of the elevated tradition of the Old Testament. And behold, Mary did not only hear these words, she did not only receive them; she gave the answer which fully responded to them: "Behold, I am the handmaid of the Lord; be it done to me

---

according to your word" (Lk. 1:38). Such an answer demanded from Mary an unconditional faith, a faith after the example of Abraham and Moses, a faith even greater than that. It is precisely this faith of Mary that Elizabeth extols.

Homily, Altotting, Germany, November 18, 1980

In the faith which Mary professed at the Annunciation as the "handmaid of the Lord" and in which she constantly "precedes" the pilgrim People of God throughout the earth, the Church "strives energetically and constantly *to bring all humanity . . . back to Christ its head in the unity of his Spirit."*

***Redemptoris Mater*, 28**

Let us meditate as we pray on the answer which Mary gave to the Annunciation. *"Fiat mihi secundum verbum tuum"* — "Let it be done unto me as you say."

***Insegnamenti*, February 1, 1981**

One must accept the call, one must listen, one must receive, one must measure one's strength, and answer "Yes, yes." Fear not, fear not, for you have found grace; do not fear life, do not fear your maternity, do not fear your marriage, do not fear your priesthood, for you have grace. This certainty, this consciousness helped us as it helped Mary.

"Earth and paradise await your 'yes,' O Virgin most pure." These are words of St. Bernard, famous, most beautiful words. They await your "yes," Mary. They await your "yes," O Mother who must give birth. A man who must take on a personal, family, social responsibility awaits your "yes." . . .

Here is Mary's response, here is the answer given by a mother, here is the reply of a young woman, a "yes" which suffices for a whole life.
Insegnamenti, **March 25, 1982**

The whole ecclesial movement of women can and should reflect the light of Gospel revelation, according to which a woman, as the representative of the human race, was called to give her consent to the Incarnation of the Word. It is the account of the Annunciation that suggests this truth when it tells that only after the *"fiat"* of Mary, who consented to be the Mother of the Messiah, did "the angel depart from her" (Lk. 1:38). The angel had completed his mission: he could bring to God humanity's "yes," spoken by Mary of Nazareth.
Address, Rome, July 13, 1994

When Mary responds to the words of the heavenly messenger with her *"fiat,"* "she who is full of grace" feels the need to express her personal relationship to the gift that has been revealed to her, saying: *"Behold, I am the handmaid of the Lord"* (Lk. 1:38). This statement should not be deprived of its profound meaning, nor should it be diminished by artificially removing it from the context of the event and from the full content of the truth revealed about God and man. In the expression "handmaid of the Lord," one senses Mary's complete awareness of being a creature of God. The word "handmaid," near the end of the Annunciation dialogue, is inscribed throughout the whole history of the Mother and Son. In fact, this Son, who is the true and consubstantial "Son of the Most High," will often say of himself, especially at the culminating moment of his mission: "The Son of Man came not to be served but to serve" (Mk. 10:45).

Mulieris Dignitatem, 5

The word of the living God, announced to Mary by an angel, referred to her: "And behold, you will conceive in your womb and bear a son"

(Lk. 1:31). By accepting this announcement, Mary was to become the "Mother of the Lord," and the divine mystery of the Incarnation was to be accomplished in her: "The Father of mercies willed that the consent of the predestined Mary should precede the Incarnation." And Mary gives this consent, after she has heard everything the messenger has to say. She says: "Behold, I am the handmaid of the Lord; let it be done to me according to your word" (Lk. 1:38). This *"fiat"* of Mary — "let it be done unto me" — was decisive, on the human level, for the accomplishment of the divine mystery. There is a complete harmony in the words of the Son, who, according to the Letter to the Hebrews, says to the Father as he comes into the world: "Sacrifices and offerings you have not desired, but a *body you have prepared for me*. . . . Lo, I have come to do your will, O God" (Heb. 10:5-7). The mystery of the Incarnation was accomplished when Mary uttered her *"fiat"*: "Let it be done unto me according to your word," which made possible, as far as it depended upon her in the divine plan, the granting of her Son's desire.

Mary uttered this *"fiat"* of faith. In faith she entrusted herself to God without reserve and "devoted herself totally as the handmaid of the Lord to the person and work of her Son." And — as the Fathers of the Church teach — she conceived this Son in her mind before she conceived him in her womb: precisely in faith! Rightly therefore does Elizabeth praise Mary: "And blessed is she who believed *that there would be a fulfillment* of what was spoken to her from the Lord." These words have already been fulfilled: Mary of Nazareth presents herself at the threshold of Elizabeth and Zachariah's house as the Mother of the Son of God. This is Elizabeth's joyful discovery: "The mother of my Lord comes to me!"

Redemptoris Mater, 13

The Blessed Virgin intoned the *Magnificat,* knowing that to accomplish the plan of salvation for all mankind, the Lord willed to bring her, a simple maiden of his people, into association with it. We are here to intone our *Magnificat,* after the example of Mary, knowing that we have been summoned by God to a service of redemption and salvation, in spite of our inadequacy.

Insegnamentl, March 19, 1982

It is my hope that in your reverence for the Word of God you will be like Mary — whose response to God's word was *"Fiat. . ."*: "Let it be done to me as you say" (Lk. 1:38); like Mary, who trusted "that the Lord's words to her would be fulfilled" (Lk. 1:45); like Mary, who treasured those things which were said of her Son and pondering them in her heart (cf. Lk. 2:19). May you treasure God's Word always and ponder it each day in your heart, so that your whole life may become a proclamation of Christ, the Word made flesh (cf. Jn. 1:14).

Address, North American College, Rome, February 22, 1980

When at the Annunciation Mary hears of the Son whose Mother she is to become and to whom "she will give the name Jesus" (i.e., Savior), she also learns that "the Lord will give to him the throne of his father David," and that "he will reign over the house of Jacob for ever and of his kingdom there will be no end" (Lk. 1:32-33). The hope of the whole of Israel was directed toward this. This promised Messiah is to be "great," and the heavenly messenger also announces that *"he will be great"* — great both by bearing the name *Son of the Most High* and by the fact that he is to assume the *inheritance of David.* He is therefore to be a king; he is to reign "over the house of Jacob." Mary had grown up in the midst of these expectations of her people: could she guess, at the moment of the Annunciation, the vital significance of the angel's words? And how is one to understand that "kingdom" which "will have no end"?

Although through faith she may have perceived in that instant that she was the Mother of the "Messiah-King," nevertheless she replied: "*Behold, I am the handmaid of the Lord*; let it be done to me according to your word" (Lk. 1:38). From the first moment, Mary professed above all the "obedience of faith," abandoning herself to the meaning which was given to the words of the Annunciation by him from whom they proceeded: God himself.

Redemptoris Mater, 15

And in the moments of weariness raise your eyes to Mary, the Virgin who, forgetting herself, set out "with haste" for the hills to reach her elderly cousin Elizabeth who was in need of help and assistance (cf. Lk. 1:39ff). Let her be the inspiration of your daily dedication to duty; let her suggest to you the right words and opportune gestures at the bedside of the sick; let her comfort you in misunderstandings and failures, hoping you always keep a smile on your face and a hope in your heart.

Address, Rome, June 18, 1979

If *through faith* Mary became the bearer of the
Son given to her by the Father through the
power of the Holy Spirit, while preserving her
virginity intact, in that same faith she
*discovered and accepted the other dimension of
motherhood* revealed by Jesus during his
messianic mission. One can say that this
dimension of motherhood belonged to Mary
from the beginning, that is, from the moment
of the conception and birth of her Son. From
that time she was "the one who believed." But
as the messianic mission of her Son grew
clearer to her eyes and spirit, she herself as a
mother became ever more open to *that new
dimension of motherhood* which was to
constitute her "part" beside her Son. Had she
not said from the very beginning: "Behold, I am
the handmaid of the Lord; let it be done to me
according to your word" (Lk. 1:38)? Through
faith Mary continued to hear and ponder that
word, in which there became ever clearer, in a
way "which surpasses knowledge" (Eph. 3:19),
the self-revelation of the living God. Thus, *in a
sense,* Mary as Mother *became the first disciple
of her Son,* the first to whom he seemed to say:
"Follow me," even before he addressed this call
to the Apostles or to anyone else (cf. Jn. 1:43).

Redemptoris Mater, 20

3 / Mary Immaculate

To *Mary Immaculate, Mother of Our Advent:*
Hail!

Blessed are you, full of grace.

Today with the greatest veneration, the Church recalls the fullness of this grace, with which God filled you from the first moment of your conception.

The Apostle's words fill us with joy, "Despite the increase of sin, grace has surpassed it" (Rom. 5:20). We are glad at this particular abundance of divine grace in you, who bear the name of "Immaculate Conception," Mother.

Accept us just as we are, here by you.

Accept us! Look into our hearts!

Accept our cares and our hopes!

Help us, you, full of grace, to live in grace, to persevere in grace and, if it should be necessary, to return to the grace of the living God, which is the greatest and supernatural good of man.

Prepare us for the advent of your Son!

Accept us with our daily problems, our weaknesses and deficiencies, our crises, and our personal, family, and social failings.

Do not let us lose good will! Do not let us lose sincerity of conscience and honesty of conduct!

Obtain justice for us through your prayer.

Save the peace of the whole world!

Be with us, you the Immaculate.

Be with us. Be with Rome. Be with the Church, and with the world. Amen.

Insegnamenti, December 8, 1979

Let us offer ourselves to God, through the Immaculate Heart of Mary, in the act of thanks and willingness; let us offer our sacrifices in union with Christ the Redeemer and, with our souls in prayer of atonement and conciliation, let us repeat: Lord Jesus, it is for love of you, in reparation for sins and for the conversion of sinners.

Address, Fátima, May 12, 1982

Blessed be God the Father of our Lord Jesus Christ, who filled you, Virgin of Nazareth, *with every spiritual blessing of Christ.* In him, you were conceived Immaculate! Predicted to be his Mother, you were redeemed in him and through him more than any other human being! Preserved from the inheritance of original sin, you were conceived and came into the world in a state of sanctifying grace. *Full of grace!*

We venerate this mystery of the faith in today's solemnity. Today, together with all the Church, we venerate the Redemption that was actuated in you. That most singular participation in the Redemption of the world and man was reserved only for you, solely for you!

Insegnamenti, December 8, 1982

Was it not for our encouragement that God chose to come to us through the Immaculate Virgin, conceived without sin? From the first moment of her existence she was never under the power of sin, while we are called to be cleansed of sin by opening our heart to the merciful Redeemer whom she brought into this world. There is no better way to approach her Son than through her.

Address, Nagasaki, February 26, 1981

I likewise invite you to turn with me to the Immaculate Heart of Mary, Mother of Jesus, in whom "is effected the reconciliation of God and humanity. . . , is accomplished the work of reconciliation, because she has received from

God the fullness of grace in virtue of the redemptive sacrifice of Christ." Truly, Mary has been associated with God, by virtue of her divine motherhood, in the work of reconciliation.

Into the hands of this Mother, whose *"fiat"* marked the beginning of that "fullness of time" in which Christ accomplished the reconciliation of humanity with God, to her Immaculate Heart — to which he has repeatedly entrusted the whole of humanity, disturbed by sin and tormented by so many tensions and conflicts — I now in a special way entrust this intention: that through her intercession humanity may discover the path of penance, the only path that can lead it to full reconciliation.

Reconciliatio et Paenitentia, 35

Consecrating the world to the Immaculate Heart of the Mother means returning beneath the cross of the Son. It means consecrating this world to the pierced heart of the Savior, bringing it back to the very source of its redemption. Redemption is always greater than man's sin and the "sin of the world." The power of the Redemption is infinitely superior to the whole range of evil in man and the world.

The heart of the Mother is aware of this, more than any other heart in the whole universe, visible and invisible.

And so she calls us.

She not only calls us to be converted: she calls us to accept her motherly help to return to the source of redemption.

Address, Fátima, May 13, 1982

We must now focus our attention on virginity and motherhood as two particular dimensions of the fulfillment of the female personality. In the light of the Gospel, they acquire their full meaning and value in Mary, who as a Virgin became the Mother of the Son of God. These *two dimensions of the female vocation* were united in her in an exceptional manner, in such a way that one did not exclude the other but wonderfully complemented it. The description of the Annunciation in the Gospel of Luke clearly shows that this seemed impossible to the Virgin of Nazareth. When she hears the words "You will conceive in your womb and bear a son, and you shall call his name Jesus," she immediately asks: "How can this be, since I have no husband?" (Lk. 1:31, 34). In the usual order of things motherhood is the result of mutual "knowledge" between a man and a woman in the marriage union.

Mary, firm in her resolve to preserve her virginity, puts this question to the divine messenger, and obtains from him the explanation: *"The Holy Spirit will come upon you"* — your motherhood will not be the consequence of matrimonial "knowledge," but will be the work of the Holy Spirit; the "power of the Most High" will "overshadow" the mystery of the Son's conception and birth; as the Son of the Most High, he is given exclusively to God, in a manner known only to God. Mary, therefore, maintained her virginal "I have no husband" (cf. Lk. 1:34) and at the same time became a mother. *Virginity and motherhood coexist in her;* they do not mutually exclude each other or place limits on each other. Indeed, the person of the Mother of God helps everyone — especially women — to see how these two dimensions, these two paths in the vocation of women as persons, explain and complete each other.

Mulieris Dignitatem, 17

The story of Lourdes is a poem of Mary's motherly love, always vigilant and concerned about her children, and it also sums up the history of so much human suffering, which has become prayer, offering confident abandonment to God's will, drawing from it comfort, serenity, meaning, and value for one's own suffering. May the Blessed Virgin, from the Grotto of Massabielle, give to you too, as to so many sick people, today and always, a smile, an encouragement, a grace that will relieve you and comfort you on your way of suffering. With these wishes I bless you.

Audience, Rome, February 11, 1981

The angel's Annunciation to Mary is framed by these reassuring words: "Do not be afraid, Mary" and "with God nothing will be impossible" (Lk. 1:30, 37). The whole of the Virgin's life is in fact pervaded by the certainty that God is near to her and that he accompanies her with his providential care. The same is true of the Church, which finds "a place prepared by God" (Rev. 12:6) in the desert, the place of trial but also of the manifestation of God's love for his people (cf. Hos. 2:16). Mary is a living word of comfort for the Church in her struggle against death. Showing us the Son, the Church assures us that in him the forces of death have already been defeated: "Death with life contended: combat strangely ended! Life's own Champion, slain, yet lives to reign."

Evangelium Vitae, **105**

Mother, I commend and entrust to you all that goes to making up earthly progress, asking that it should not be one-sided, but that it should create conditions for the full spiritual advancement of individuals, families, communities, and nations. I commend to you the poor, the suffering, the sick and the handicapped, the aging and the dying. I ask you to reconcile those in sin, to heal those in pain, and to uplift those who have lost their hope and joy. Show to those who struggle in doubt the light of Christ your Son.

Bishops of the Church in the United States have chosen your Immaculate Conception as the mystery to hold the patronage over the People of God in this land. May the hope contained in this mystery overcome sin and be shared by all the sons and daughters of America, and also by the whole human family. At a time when the struggle between good and evil, between the prince of darkness and father of lies and evangelical love is growing more acute, may the light of your Immaculate Conception show to all the way to grace and to salvation. Amen.

Address, Immaculate Conception Shrine, Washington, D.C., October 7, 1979

On the feast of the Annunciation in this Holy Year of the Redemption, I place the present exhortation *in the heart of the Immaculate Virgin.* Among all persons consecrated unreservedly to God, she is the first. She — the Virgin of Nazareth — is also one of the *most fully consecrated to God,* consecrated in the most perfect way. Her spousal love reached its height in the divine motherhood through the power of the Holy Spirit. She, who as Mother carries Christ in her arms, at the same time *fulfills* in the most perfect way *his call:* "Follow me." And she follows him — she, the Mother — as her Teacher of chastity, poverty, and obedience.

How poor she was on Bethlehem night and how poor on Calvary! How *obedient* she was at the moment of the Annunciation, and then — at the foot of the cross — *obedient* even to the point of assenting to the death of her Son, who became obedient "unto death"! How *dedicated* she was in all her earthly life to the cause of the kingdom of heaven *through most chaste love.*

Redemptionis Donum, 17

And stay close also to our Blessed Mother Mary and her Immaculate Heart. When Mary said "Yes" to the angel, the mystery of Redemption took shape beneath her heart.

The pure heart of Mary was the inspiration for many of the missionaries who brought the Word of God to the African people. And for the Church today this heart of Mary continues to express the mystery of the Mother in redemption (cf. *Redemptor Hominis*, 22).

In the name of Jesus, I bless you all. And I commend you and your families and friends to Mary, who is the Mother of us all.

Address, Kumasi, Ghana, May 9, 1980

While we are preparing ourselves for the solemnity of Holy Mary's Assumption into heaven, I entrust to her your intentions of perseverance! Mary, who is our Mother, points out to us the goal of heaven toward which we are aiming, day by day. Pray to her with deep devotion: her tender love has the wonderful power to transform the painful mysteries, which sometimes sadden our lives, into joyful mysteries transfigured by love. I grant now to all of you my affectionate and conciliatory blessing.

Address, Castel Gandolfo, August 12, 1980

Dearest ones, while I thank you heartily for your presence here, I call your attention to the imminent feast of our Lady assumed into heaven. We know that Mary Immaculate, Spouse of the Holy Spirit, Mother of Christ and the Church, first of the redeemed, at the end of her life on earth was raised in spirit and body to heavenly glory. Such an admirable event teaches that man's destiny is not consumed with time, but is projected and completed in heaven, beside God.

Audience, Rome, August 20, 1980

The teachings of my predecessor Paul VI will never be forgotten; in his stupendous Apostolic Exhortations *Signum Magnum* and *Marialis Cultus*, he left a monument of his devotion and love for Mary, and a complete synthesis of biblical, theological, and liturgical motives that must guide the People of God in the continual growth of the veneration owed to her who is the Mother of God, our Mother, and Mother of the Church.

Also in the ecumenical sphere, especially in relations with sister Churches of the East, this inspiration to renewal comes to us from confidence in the intercession of Mary, who considers us all her children, in which we can find a strong impetus to a unity which, in devotion to Mary, we already find realized.

Address, Rome, Feast of Sts. Peter and Paul, 1980

It is especially in Mary, Mother of God and Mother of the Church, that religious life comes to understand itself most deeply and finds its sign of certain hope (cf. *Lumen Gentium*, 68). She, who was conceived immaculate because she was called from among God's people to bear God himself most intimately and to give him to the world, was consecrated totally by the overshadowing of the Holy Spirit. She was the Ark of the New Covenant itself. The handmaid of the Lord in the poverty of the *anawim*, the Mother of fair love from Bethlehem to Calvary and beyond, the obedient virgin whose "yes" to God changed our history, the contemplative who kept all of these things in her heart, the missionary hurrying to Hebron, the one who was sensitive to the needs at Cana, the steadfast witness at the foot of the cross, the center of unity which held the young Church together in its expectation of the Holy Spirit — Mary showed throughout her life all those values to which religious consecration is directed. She is the

Mother of religious in being Mother of him who was consecrated, sent, and in her *"fiat"* and *Magnificat* religious life finds the totality of its surrender to and the thrill of its joy in the consecratory action of God.

> **Essential Elements in the Church's Teaching on the Religious Life. . . , 53**

4 / Mediatrix of All Graces

O Mother of men and peoples, you know all their sufferings and hopes, you maternally feel all their struggles between good and evil, between the light and the darkness which shake the world. Receive our cry, directed in the Holy Spirit straight to your heart and, with the love of the Mother and the handmaid of the Lord, embrace the individuals and peoples which most look for the embrace, together with the individuals and peoples to whose trust you attend in a particular way. Take the entire human family under your maternal protection. With outflows of affections, O Mother, we entrust it to you. May the time of peace and liberty approach for all, the time of truth, justice, and hope.

Insegnamenti, May 9, 1982

As the Council says, "Mary figured prominently in the history of salvation. . . . Hence when she is being preached and venerated, she summons the faithful to her Son and his sacrifice, and to love for the Father." For this reason, Mary's faith, according to the Church's apostolic witness, in some ways continues to become the faith of the pilgrim People of God: the faith of individuals and communities, of places and gatherings, and of the various groups existing in the Church. It is a faith that is passed simultaneously through both the mind and heart. It is gained or regained through prayer. Therefore, *"the Church* in her apostolic work also *rightly looks to her who brought forth Christ,* conceived by the Holy Spirit and born of the Virgin, so that through the Church Christ *may be born and increase in the hearts of the faithful also."*

Redemptoris Mater, 28

When greeting Mary, Elizabeth in no way separated Mother and Son. Rather did she associate them intimately, for she added, *"and blest is the fruit of your womb."* So, we too must address ourselves to the Lord Jesus with the readiness of lively faith, with the force of ardent love. The content of the expression *"Ad Iesum per Mariam"* ("To Jesus through Mary") must be shown to be true for us too, that is, that it is really fact. . . .

Insegnamenti, February 11, 1982

Courage, dearest brothers and sisters. *The world is thirsty, even without knowing it, for the Divine Mercy,* and you are called to proffer this prodigious water, healing to soul and body. You venerate the Mother of Mercy under the particular title "Mary Mediatrix." May she make you even more conscious of her motherhood, "which endures without cease from the moment of the consent faithfully given to the Annunciation," and may she make you all apostles, workers, and servers of the Divine Goodness and Mercy. I accompany you with my blessing.

Insegnamenti, January 2, 1981

"When the time had fully come, *God sent forth his Son, born of woman.*" With these words of his Letter to the Galatians (4:4), the Apostle Paul links together the principal moments which essentially determine the fulfillment of the mystery "predetermined in God" (cf. Eph. 1:9). The Son, the Word, one in substance with the Father, becomes man, born of a woman, at the fullness of time. This event leads *to the turning point* of man's history on earth, understood as salvation history. It is significant that St. Paul does not call the

Mother of Christ by her own name, "Mary," but calls her "woman": this coincides with the words of the Proto-evangelium in the Book of Genesis (cf. 3:15). She is that "woman" who is present in the central salvific event which marks the "fullness of time": this event is realized in her and through her.

Mulieris Dignitatem, 3

The divine plan of salvation — which was fully revealed to us with the coming of Christ is eternal. And according to the teaching in the Letter [to the Ephesians] . . . and in other Pauline Letters (cf. Col. 1:12-14; Rom. 3:24; Gal. 3:13), it is also *eternally linked to Christ.* It includes everyone, but it reserves a special place for the *"woman"* who is the Mother of him to whom the Father has entrusted the work of salvation. As the Second Vatican Council says, "She is already prophetically foreshadowed in that promise made to our first parents after their fall into sin" — according to the Book of Genesis (cf. 3:15). Likewise she is the Virgin who is to conceive and bear a son, who shall be called Emmanuel — according to the words of Isaiah (cf. 7:14). In this way the Old Testament prepares that "fullness of time" when God sent forth his Son, "born of a woman . . . so that we might receive adoption as sons." The coming into the world of the Son of God is an event recorded in the first chapters of the Gospels according to Luke and Matthew.

Redemptoris Mater, 7

Dear sick people, I call upon you to address a thought of fervent devotion to Mary, the joy of our hearts, the consoler of all those who suffer. Even if we are tried by pain, we cannot but rejoice in our God, who has clothed us with the garments of salvation and with the robes of righteousness (cf. Is. 61:10), in order to be able to change our suffering into a loving offer, in imitation of our Lady, the co-redeemer. May Mary nourish in you sentiments of sincerity and hope, and may she strengthen also the blessing, which I impart upon you from the bottom of my heart.

Audience, Rome, December 10, 1980

Upright by the cross of her Son on Calvary, the most holy Virgin shared in his Passion and knows how to convince ever fresh souls to unite their suffering with Christ's sacrifice, in a joint "offertory," which surpasses time and space and embraces the whole of mankind and saves it.

Insegnamenti, February 11, 1980

Consecrating oneself to Mary means helping her to offer ourselves and mankind to him who is holy, infinitely holy; it means letting oneself be aided by her — by having recourse to her Mother's heart, opened beneath the cross to love for every person, for the whole world — to offer the world and man, and mankind, and all nations to him who is infinitely holy. God's holiness was manifested in the redemption of man, of the world, of the whole of mankind, of the nations: a redemption which occurred through the sacrifice of the cross. "I consecrate myself for their sakes," Jesus said (Jn. 17:19).

The world and man *were consecrated through the power of the Redemption.* They were consecrated to him who is infinitely holy. They were offered and confided to Love himself, to the merciful Love.

The Mother of Christ summons us and invites us to join with the Church of the living God *in this consecration of the world,* in this entrustment whereby the world, mankind, the nations, all individual people are offered to the eternal Father through the power of the Redemption of Christ. They are offered up in the heart of the Redeemer pierced on the cross.

The Mother of the Redeemer calls us, asks us, and aids us to join in this consecration, in entrustment of the world. Then indeed do we find ourselves as near as possible to the heart of Christ pierced on the cross.

Insegnamenti, May 13, 1982

Dear brothers, always remember that the Mother of Jesus is here; she is with us today, and she will continue to be with you in your preparation for future mission at home. She will accompany you on your mission of evangelization throughout your land. Act on her words; listen to Jesus as he invites you to a great intimacy with himself, union with your bishops, and a renewed dedication to generous and faithful celibate love in the service of evangelization. It will always be so. Wherever you are, you can say: the Mother of Christ is here!

Address, Rome, January 30, 1982

I commend all of you to the Virgin Mary, Mother and model for every consecrated soul. May she make abundant vocations to the consecrated life flourish, for the greater glory of God, the good of the Church, and the service of love and humanity. And may the Lord always keep you faithful to your vocation. In his name I bless you with all my heart.

Address, Quito, January 30, 1985

"The Almighty has done great things for me,"
Mary declared. She was fully aware of the
greatness of her mission; but at the same time,
she recognized herself to be and remained, "a
lowly servant," attributing all glory to God the
Savior. The grandeur of the redemptive mission
is accomplished in Mary through the perfect
accord between divine omnipotence and
humble human docility.

Insegnamenti, March 19, 1982

Everything begins with the conversation
between the Virgin and the Archangel Gabriel:
"How shall this be, since I have no husband?"
(Lk. 1:34). Answer: "The Holy Spirit will come
upon you, and the power of the Most High will
overshadow you: there the child to be born will
be called holy, the Son of God" (Lk. 1:35). At
the same time as physical motherhood, Mary's
spiritual motherhood began, a motherhood
which filled the nine months of waiting, but
which was prolonged also beyond the moment
of the birth of Jesus to embrace the thirty
years spent between Bethlehem, Egypt, and
Nazareth, and then also the years of Jesus'
public life, when the Son of Mary left his home
in Nazareth to preach the Gospel of the
kingdom: years which culminated in Calvary

and in the supreme sacrifice on the cross.

It was here, under the cross, that Mary's spiritual motherhood reached its key moment, in a certain sense. When Jesus saw his Mother and the disciple whom he loved standing near, he said to his Mother, "Woman, behold your son!" (Jn. 19:26). Thus Jesus linked Mary, his Mother, in a new way with man, to whom he had given the Gospel.

Jesus linked her, then, with every man, as he united her, subsequently, with the Church, on the day of its historic birth, that is, the day of Pentecost. From that day, the whole Church had her as Mother, and all men have her as Mother. They understand the words spoken from the cross, as addressed to each of them. Spiritual motherhood knows no limits; it extends in time and space, and reaches all human hearts. It reaches whole nations and becomes the keystone of human culture. Motherhood: a great, splendid, fundamental human reality, present at the beginning of time in the Creator's plan, solemnly reconfirmed in the mystery of the birth of God, with which it now remains inseparably linked.

Address, Rome, January 10, 1979

I wish to place you under the protection of the Blessed Virgin. May she, who for many years could profit from the visible presence of Jesus and who treated her Divine Son with the greatest care and delicacy, accompany you always to the Eucharist. May she give you her own sentiments of adoration and of love.

Address, Castel Gandolfo, August 19, 1979

Simeon said to Mary, Mother of Jesus: "And you yourself shall be pierced with a sword!"

Dear brothers and sisters! Receive Christ from the hands of Mary! May the mystery of the Redemption reach you through her soul! May all the salvific plans of consecrated hearts always be manifest before the heart of the Mother! United with her. With your glance focused on her. In her there is a special resemblance to Christ, the Spouse of your souls.

Homily, Rome, February 2, 1984

During the banquet at Cana in Galilee, Mary asked the first sign from her Son on behalf of those newlyweds and those in charge of the house. Mary does not cease to pray for you, for all the young people of Poland and of the whole world, so that there will be manifested in you the sign of the new presence of Christ in history.

And you, my dearest friends, remember well these words which the Mother of Christ spoke at Cana, turning to those who were to fill the water jars. She said then, pointing to her Son, "Do whatever he tells you!" (Jn. 2:5).

To you also she says the same thing today.

Accept these words.

Remember them.

Put them into practice.

Address, Jasna Góra, July 6, 1979

At Cana in Galilee, there is shown only one concrete aspect of human need, apparently a small one of little importance ("They have no wine"). But it has a symbolic value: this coming to the aid of human need means, at the same time, bringing those needs within the radius of Christ's messianic mission and salvific power. Thus there is mediation: Mary places herself between her Son and mankind in the reality of their wants, needs, and sufferings. *She puts herself "in the middle," that is to say, she acts as a mediatrix and not as an outsider, but in her position as Mother.* She knows that as such she can point out to her Son the needs of mankind, and in fact, she "has the right" to do so. Her mediation is thus in the nature of intercession. Mary "intercedes" for mankind. And that is not all. As a mother, she also *wishes the messianic power of her Son to be manifested* and that salvific power of his which is meant to help man in his misfortunes, to free him from the evil which in various forms and degrees weighs heavily upon his life. Precisely as the Prophet Isaiah foretold about the Messiah in the famous passage which Jesus quoted before his fellow townsfolk in Nazareth: "To preach good news to the poor . . . to proclaim release to the captives and recovering the sight of the blind. . ." (cf. Lk. 4:18).

Redemptoris Mater, 21

My first desire, in this National Shrine of the Immaculate Conception, is to direct my thoughts, to turn my heart to the woman of salvation history. In the eternal design of God, this woman, Mary, was chosen to enter into the work of the Incarnation and Redemption. This design of God was to be actuated through her free decision given in obedience to the divine will. Through her "yes," a "yes" that pervades and is reflected in all history, she consented to be the Virgin Mother of our saving God, the handmaid of the Lord, and at the same time the Mother of all the faithful who in the course of the centuries would become brothers and sisters of her Son.

Through her, the Sun of justice was to rise in the world. Through her the great Healer of humanity, the Reconciler of hearts and consciences, her Son, the God-Man, Jesus Christ, was to transform the human condition and by his death and resurrection uplift the entire human family. As a great sign that appeared in the heavens, in the fullness of time, the woman dominates all history as the Virgin Mother of the Son and as the spouse of the Holy Spirit, as the handmaid of humanity.

Address, Washington, D.C., October 7, 1979

"*Standing by the cross of Jesus* were his mother, and his mother's sister, Mary the wife of Clopas, and Mary Magdalene. When Jesus saw his mother, and the disciple whom he loved standing near, he said to his mother: 'Woman, behold your son!' Then he said to the disciple: 'Behold your mother!' And from that hour the disciple took her to his own home" (Jn. 19:25-27).

Undoubtedly, we find here an expression of the Son's particular solicitude for his Mother, whom he is leaving in such great sorrow. And yet the "testament of Christ's cross" says more. Jesus highlights a new relationship between Mother and Son, the whole truth and reality of which he solemnly confirms. One can say that if Mary's motherhood of the human race has already been outlined, now it is clearly stated and established. It *emerges* from the definitive accomplishment of *the Redeemer's Paschal Mystery*. The Mother of Christ, who stands at the very center of the mystery — a mystery which embraces each individual and all humanity — is given as Mother to every single individual and all mankind. The man at the foot of the cross is John, "the disciple whom he loved." But it is not he alone. Following tradition, the Council does not hesitate to call Mary *"the Mother of Christ and mother of mankind"*: since she "belongs to the offspring of Adam she is one with all human beings. . . . Indeed she is 'clearly the mother of the members of Christ . . . since she cooperated out of love so that there might be born into the Church the faithful.' "

Redemptoris Mater, 23

5 / Mirror of Perfection

Dear ordinands, dear priests, at this point my address becomes a prayer, a prayer which I wish to entrust to the intercession of the Blessed Virgin, the Mother of the Church and Queen of the Apostles. In your anxious expectation of the priesthood, you certainly took your place near her, like the Apostles in the Upper Room. May she obtain for you the graces you most need for your sanctification and for the religious prosperity of your country. May she grant you especially love — the love that gave her the grace of generating Christ — in order to be capable of carrying out your mission of generating Christ in souls, too. May she teach you to be pure, as she was; may she make you faithful to the divine call, and make you understand the whole beauty, joy, and power of a ministry lived unreservedly in dedication and immolation for the service of God and of souls. Finally, let us ask Mary, for you and for all of us here present, to help us to say, following her example, the great word "yes," to the will of God, even when it is demanding, even when it is perhaps incomprehensible, even when it is painful for us. Amen.

Homily to priests, Rio de Janeiro, July 2, 1980

Such was the case, as the Gospel recounts, with Mary and Joseph who, at the threshold of the New Covenant, renewed the experience of "fairest love" described in the Song of Solomon. Joseph thinks of Mary in the words: "My sister, my bride" (Song 4:9). Mary, the Mother of God, conceived [Jesus] by the power of the Holy Spirit, who is in the origin of the "fairest love," which the Gospel delicately places in the context of the "great mystery."

When we speak about "fairest love," we are also speaking about beauty: the beauty of love and the beauty of the human being who, by the power of the Holy Spirit, is capable of such love. We are speaking of the beauty of man and woman: their beauty as brother or sister, as a couple about to be married, as husband and wife. The Gospel sheds light not only on the mystery of "fairest love," but also on the equally profound mystery of beauty, which, like love, is from God. Man and woman are from God, two persons called to become a mutual gift. From the primordial gift of the Spirit, the "giver of life," there arises the reciprocal gift of being husband or wife, no less that of brother or sister.

All this is confirmed by the mystery of the Incarnation, a mystery which has been *the source of a new beauty* in the history of humanity and has inspired countless masterpieces of art.

Letter to Families, February 22, 1994

Mary most holy, the highly favored daughter of the Father, will appear before the eyes of the believers as the perfect model of love toward both God and neighbor. As she herself says in the canticle of the *Magnificat*, great things were done for her by the Almighty, whose name is holy (cf. Lk. 1:49). The Father chose her for a unique mission in the history of salvation: that of being the Mother of the long-awaited Savior. The Virgin Mary responds to God's call with complete openness: "Behold, I am the handmaid of the Lord" (Lk. 1:38). Her motherhood, which began in Nazareth and was lived most intensely in Jerusalem at the foot of the cross, will be felt . . . as a loving and urgent invitation addressed to all the children of God so that they will return to the house of the Father when they hear her maternal voice: "Do whatever Christ tells you" (cf. Jn. 2:5).

Tertio Millennio Adveniente, 54

In the tradition of faith and of Christian
reflection throughout the ages, *the coupling
Adam-Christ* is often linked with that of *Eve-
Mary.* If Mary is described as the "new-Eve,"
what are the meanings of this analogy?
Certainly there are many. Particularly
noteworthy is the meaning which sees Mary as
the full revelation of all that is included in the
biblical word "woman": a revelation
commensurate with the mystery of
Redemption. *Mary* means, in a sense, going
beyond the limit spoken of in the Book of
Genesis (3:16) and a return to that "beginning"
in which one finds the "woman" as she was
intended to be in *creation,* and therefore in the
eternal mind of God: in the bosom of the most
holy Trinity. Mary is "the new beginning" of the
dignity and vocation of women, of each and
every woman.

A particular key for understanding this can
be found in the words which the Evangelist
puts on Mary's lips after the Annunciation
during her visit to Elizabeth: "He who is mighty
has done great things for me" (Lk. 1:49). These
words certainly refer to the conception of her
Son, who is "the Son of the Most High" (Lk.
1:32), the "holy one" of God; but they can also
signify *the discovery of her own feminine
humanity. He "has done great things for me":*

this is *the discovery of all the richness and personal resources of femininity*, all the eternal originality of the "woman" just as God wanted her to be, a person for her own sake, who discovers herself "by means of a sincere gift of self."

This discovery is connected with a clear awareness of God's gift, of his generosity. From the very "beginning" sin had obscured this awareness, in a sense had stifled it, as is shown in the words of the first temptation by the "father of lies" (cf. Gen. 3:1-5). At the advent of the "fullness of time" (cf. Gal. 4:4), when the mystery of Redemption begins to be fulfilled in the history of humanity, this awareness bursts forth in all its power in the words of the biblical "woman" of Nazareth. In Mary, Eve discovers the nature of the true dignity of woman, of feminine humanity. This discovery must continually reach the heart of every woman and shape her vocation and her life.

Mulieris Dignitatem, 11

The Annunciation, therefore, is the revelation of the mystery of the Incarnation at the very beginning of its fulfillment on earth. God's salvific giving of himself and his life, in some ways to all creation but directly to man, reaches *one of its high points in the mystery of the Incarnation*. This is indeed a high point among all gifts of grace conferred in the history of man and of the universe: Mary is "full of grace," because it is precisely in her that the Incarnation of the Word, the hypostatic union of the Son of God with human nature, is accomplished and fulfilled. As the Council says, Mary is "the Mother of the Son of God. As a result she is also the favorite daughter of the Father and the temple of the Holy Spirit. Because of this gift of sublime grace, she far surpasses all other creatures, both in heaven and on earth."

Redemptoris Mater, 9

In creating the human race "male and female," God gives man and woman an equal personal dignity, endowing them with the inalienable rights and responsibilities proper to the human person. God then manifests the dignity of women in the highest form possible, by assuming human flesh from the Virgin Mary, whom the Church honors as the Mother of God, calling her the new Eve and presenting her as the model of redeemed woman.

Familiaris Consortio, 22

Mary is also she who, in a particular and exceptional way — unlike any other — experienced mercy, and at the same time, always in an exceptional way, made her participation in the revelation of the divine mercy possible with the sacrifice of her heart. Such sacrifice is closely bound up with the cross of her Son, at the foot of which she was to stand at Calvary. That sacrifice of hers was a singular participation in revelation of mercy, that is, of God's own absolute fidelity to his own love, to the alliance which he had willed to make from all eternity and which he concluded in time with man, with the people, with mankind. It was participation in that revelation which was definitively accomplished through the cross.

No one has experienced the mystery of the cross as did the Mother of the Crucified — the astounding encounter between transcendent divine justice and love, that "kiss" which mercy gave to justice (cf. Ps. 85:11). No one on the same level as you, Mary, has taken that mystery into the heart, that truly divine dimension of the Redemption, which actuated on Calvary through the death of the Son, together with the sacrifice of your motherly heart, with your definitive "*fiat* — let it be done. . . ."

Address, Rome, November 30, 1980

A word about Mary, the Mother of Jesus and Mother of the Church, to whose loving patronage God himself willed to entrust, through her obedient "yes," the fate of the whole of mankind. The Son assigns to her the motherly task of imploring individual and collective salvation for us.

Dear young people, the revival, in the present time, of true Christian values such as brotherhood, justice, and peace, is entrusted once more to the intervention and motherly pedagogy of Mary. For today, too, she is Mother of divine grace; she is Queen of Victories.

Audience, Rome, May 5, 1979

The Blessed Virgin Mary, the first of the redeemed, the first to have been closely associated with the work of Redemption, will always be your guide and model.

Audience, Rome, May 13, 1983

Finally, always maintain a tender devotion to the holy Mother of God. Your piety for her should retain the simplicity of its first moments. May the Mother of Jesus, who is also our Mother, model of surrender to the

Lord and to his mission, accompany you, in whatever circumstances of your life, that you may have the joy and unalterable peace which only the Lord can give. In pledge of this, I affectionately impart to you my cordial blessing.

Address, Ávila, Spain, November 4, 1982

And now, standing at the foot of the cross, Mary is the witness, humanly speaking, of the complete *negation of these words* ["He will be great . . . and the Lord God will give him the throne of David . . . and of his kingdom there will be no end" (Lk. 1:32-33)]. On that wood of the cross her Son hangs in agony as one condemned. "He was despised and rejected by men; a man of sorrows . . . he was despised, and we esteemed him not": as one destroyed (cf. Is. 53:3-5). How great, how heroic then is the *obedience of faith* shown by Mary in the face of God's "unsearchable judgments"! How completely she "abandons herself to God" without reserve, "offering the full assent of the intellect and the will" to him whose "ways are inscrutable" (cf. Rom. 11:33)! And how powerful, too, is the action of grace in her soul, how all-pervading is the influence of the Holy Spirit and his light and power!

Redemptoris Mater, 18

If the entire Church finds in Mary her *first model,* all the more reason do you find her so — you as consecrated individuals and communities within the Church! On the day that calls to mind the inauguration of the Jubilee of the Redemption, which took place last year, I address myself to you with this present message, to invite you to renew *your religious consecration according to the model of the consecration of the very Mother of God.*

Beloved brothers and sisters! "God is faithful, by whom you were called into the fellowship of his Son, Jesus Christ our Lord." Persevering in fidelity to him who is faithful, strive to find a very special *support in Mary!* For she was called by God to the most perfect communion with his Son. May she, the faithful Virgin, also be the Mother of your evangelical way; may she help you to experience and to show to the world *how infinitely faithful is God himself!*

Redemptionis Donum, 17

Through this faith Mary is perfectly united with Christ in his self-emptying. For "Christ Jesus, who, though he was in the form of God, did not count equality with God a thing to be grasped, but emptied himself, taking the form of a servant, being born in the likeness of men": precisely on Golgotha he "humbled himself and became obedient unto death, even death on a cross" (cf. Phil. 2:5-8). At the foot of the cross Mary shares through faith in the shocking mystery of this self-emptying. This is perhaps the deepest *"kenosis" of faith* in human history. Through faith the Mother shares in the death of her Son, in his redeeming death; but in contrast with the faith of the disciples who fled, hers was far more enlightened. On Golgotha, Jesus through the cross definitively confirmed that he was the "sign of contradiction" foretold by Simeon. At the same time, there were also fulfilled on Golgotha the words which Simeon had addressed to Mary: "and a sword will pierce through your own soul also."

Redemptoris Mater, 18

The Church perseveres in prayer with Mary. This union of the praying Church with the Mother of Christ has been part of the mystery of the Church from the beginning: we see her present in this mystery as she is present in the mystery of her Son. It is the Council that says to us: "The Blessed Virgin . . . overshadowed by the Holy Spirit . . . brought forth . . . the Son

. . . , he whom God placed as the firstborn among many brethren (cf. Rom. 8:29), namely the faithful. In their birth and development she cooperates with a maternal love"; she is through "his singular graces and offices . . . intimately united with the Church. . . . [She] is a model of the Church." "The Church, moreover, contemplating Mary's mysterious sanctity, imitating her charity, . . . *becomes herself a mother*" and "herself is a virgin, who keeps . . . the fidelity she has pledged to her Spouse. Imitating the Mother of the Lord, and by the power of the Holy Spirit, she preserves with virginal purity an integral faith, a firm hope, and a sincere charity."

Dominum et Vivificantem, 6

We will be able to sing the *Magnificat* with interior exultation of spirit, if we seek to have within us Mary's sentiments: her faith, her humility, her purity. There is a beautiful expression of Ambrose, with which the holy bishop of Milan specifically exhorts us to this: "Let Mary's soul," he says, "magnify the Lord in each one; let Mary's spirit exalt God in each one; if, according to the flesh, the Mother of Christ is one only, according to the faith all souls beget Christ; for each one receives the Word of God in it, provided that it preserves chastity with unblemished modesty, keeping itself spotless and free from sin" (*Expos. Ev. sec. Lucam.* II, 26).

Homily, Rome, February 11, 1981

6 / Mother of the Church

Hail Mary, Mother of Christ and of the Church!
Hail our life, our sweetness, and our hope!

To your care I entrust the necessities of all
families, the joys of children, the desires of the
young, the worries of adults, the pain of the
sick, the serene old age of senior citizens! I
entrust to you the fidelity of your Son's
ministers, the hope of all those preparing
themselves for this ministry, the joyous
dedication of virgins in cloisters, the prayer
and concern of men and women religious, the
lives and the commitment of all those who
work for Christ's reign on earth.

Insegnamenti, **December 31, 1979**

Mary to whom we have come today as pilgrims
. . . carries the features of that woman whom
the Apocalypse describes: "A woman adorned
with the sun, standing on the moon, and with
twelve stars on her head for a crown" (Rev.
12:1). The woman, who stands at the end of
the history of creation and salvation,

corresponds evidently to the one about whom it is said in the first pages of the Bible that she "is going to crush the head of the serpent."

Between this promising beginning and the apocalyptic end, Mary has brought to light a Son "who is to rule all nations with an iron scepter" (Rev. 12:5).

Her heel it is which is being persecuted by that first "serpent." She it is with whom the apocalyptic dragon makes war; for being the Mother of the redeemed, she is the image of the Church whom we likewise call Mother (cf. *Lumen Gentium*, 68).

Address, Altotting, Germany, November 18, 1980

The words uttered by Jesus from the cross signifying the *motherhood* of her who bore Christ finds a "new" continuation *in the Church and through the Church,* symbolized and represented by John. In this way, she who as the one "full of grace" was brought into the mystery of Christ in order to be his Mother and *the Holy Mother of God*, through the Church remains in that mystery as *"the woman"* spoken of by the Book of Genesis (3:15) at the beginning, and by the Apocalypse (12:1) at the end of the history of salvation. In accordance with the eternal plan of Providence, Mary's divine motherhood is to be poured out upon the Church, as indicated by statements of tradition, according to which Mary's "motherhood" of the Church is the reflection and extension of her motherhood of the Son of God.

Redemptoris Mater, 24

The Second Vatican Council itself shed light on the outstanding place of Mary in the mystery of Christ and the Church and venerates her as "preeminent and as a wholly unique member of the Church, and as its type and outstanding model in faith and charity. The Catholic Church, taught by the Holy Spirit, honors her with filial affection and devotion as a most beloved Mother" (*Lumen Gentium*, 53).

Audience, Rome, November 28, 1980

Motherhood means concern for the life of the child. Now, if Mary is the Mother of all mankind, then her concern for the life of man *has universal extension.* Mary's maternity has its beginning in her maternal care for Christ. In Christ, she accepted John beneath the cross, and, in him, *she accepted every human and all humanity.* Mary embraces all with a particular solicitude in the Holy Spirit.

Insegnamenti, May 13, 1982

At this hour, here at the shrine of Fátima, I
wish to repeat now, before you all, *totus tuus* —
all yours, O Mother! I ask you to offer me and
all these brethren up to the "Father of
Mercies," in homage and gratitude, hiding and
covering our poverty with your merits and
those of your Divine Son. And may we be
accepted, blessed, and strengthened in our
good resolves, which we wish to bind up, like a
bunch of flowers, with a ribbon "woven and
gilded" for you, O Mother: "Do whatever he
tells you."

Give us your blessing, Lady, our most
beloved Mother!

Insegnamenti, May 12, 1982

I desire to make reference in this way to the act
which Pope Pius XII performed forty and thirty
years ago and which was recalled also by Pope
Paul VI, when he proclaimed Mary "Mother of
the Church" on the occasion of the closure of
the third session of the Council.

The contemporary world is threatened in
various ways. It is perhaps threatened more
than it has been at any other time in the
course of history. So it is necessary for the
Church to wake and watch at the feet of him
who is the sole Lord of history and Prince of

the age to come. I therefore desire *to watch and wake together with the whole Church,* raising a cry to the heart of the Immaculate Mother.

I invite all to join with me in spirit.

Insegnamenti, May 9, 1982

On the cross Christ said: "Woman, behold your son!" With these words he opened in a new way his Mother's heart. A little later, the Roman soldier's spear pierced the side of the Crucified One. That pierced heart became a sign of the Redemption achieved through the death of the Lamb of God.

The Immaculate Heart of Mary — opened with the words "Woman, behold, your son!" — is spiritually united with the heart of her Son, opened by the soldier's spear. Mary's heart was opened by the same love for man and for the world with which Christ loved man and the world, offering himself for them on the cross, until the soldier's spear struck that blow.

Consecrating the world to the Immaculate Heart of Mary means drawing near, through the Mother's intercession, to the very Fountain of Life that sprang from Golgotha. This Fountain pours forth unceasingly redemption and grace. In it reparation is made consensually for the sins of the world. It is a ceaseless source of new life and holiness.

Address, Fátima, May 13, 1982

The Second Vatican Council devoted the last chapter of its *Lumen Gentium* to the Mother of God as Mother of the Church, and speaks of her special presence in the life of the faithful an analogy with her presence in Christ's life. I cannot close my address to the College of Cardinals without giving witness to Mary's own motherly presence, which I have experienced throughout my life, especially as Bishop of Rome. At this time, my thoughts go on pilgrimage to the Marian shrines of the world that I have been able to visit. It is a pilgrimage that begins at the Shrine of Our Lady of Guadalupe in Mexico. From there I started the journey of my Petrine ministry, later taking the road that led to the heart of North and South America. As for the European continent, we all continually pore over the message of Our Lady of Lourdes, which is an exhortation to prayer and conversion, and the tears of Our Lady of La Salette as we face the great spiritual dangers of our time. I had the personal opportunity to understand the message of Our Lady of Fátima in a particular way: the first time on May 13, 1981, when an attempt was made on the pope's life, and then again toward the end of the 1980s when communism collapsed in the countries of the Soviet bloc. I think it is a sufficiently clear experience for everyone. We trust that the Blessed Virgin, who goes before the pilgrim People of God through history, will help us to surmount the difficulties that since 1989 are still present in the countries of Europe and of other continents. We are confident that the Mother of God will help us overcome all dangers, especially those that have appeared during the conflict in the Balkans. We also entrust ourselves to her intercession for the task of making peace flourish again in the African countries sorely tried by fratricidal wars. In particular, we recommend to her the land of Rwanda, asking her to assist the inhabitants on the road to reconciliation and the return of solidarity and cooperation.

"Preparing for the Great Jubilee of the Year 2000," June 13, 1994

The Blessed Virgin . . . will be contemplated especially in the mystery of her divine motherhood. It was in her womb that the Word became flesh! The affirmation of the central place of Christ cannot therefore be separated from the recognition of the role played by his most holy Mother. Veneration of her, when properly understood, can in no way take away from the "dignity and efficacy of Christ the one Mediator." Mary, in fact, constantly points to her Divine Son and she is proposed to all believers as the model of faith which is put into practice. "Devotedly meditating on her and contemplating her in the light of the Word made man, the Church with reverence enters more intimately into the supreme mystery of the Incarnation and becomes ever increasingly like her spouse."

Tertio Millennio Adveniente, 43

The same analogy — and the same truth — are present in the *Dogmatic Constitution of the Church*. Mary is *the "figure" of the Church:* "For in the mystery of the Church, herself rightly called mother and virgin, the Blessed Virgin came first as an eminent and singular exemplar of both virginity and motherhood. . . . The Son whom she brought forth is he whom God placed as the firstborn among many brethren (cf. Rom. 8:29), namely, among the faithful. In their birth and development she cooperates with a maternal love." "Moreover, contemplating Mary's mysterious sanctity, imitating her charity, and faithfully fulfilling the Father's will, the Church *herself becomes a mother* by accepting God's word in faith. For by her preaching and by baptism she brings forth a new and immortal life for children who are

conceived by the Holy Spirit and born of God."
This is motherhood "according to the Spirit"
with regard to the sons and daughters of the
human race. And this motherhood — as
already mentioned — becomes the woman's
"role" also in virginity. The Church *herself is a
virgin*, who keeps whole and pure the fidelity
she has pledged to her Spouse. This is most
perfectly fulfilled in Mary. The Church,
therefore, "imitating the Mother of her Lord,
and by the power of the Holy Spirit, preserves
with virginal purity an integral faith, firm hope,
and a sincere charity."

The Council has confirmed that, unless
one looks to the Mother of God, it is impossible
to understand the mystery of the Church, her
reality, her essential vitality. Indirectly we find
here *a reference to the biblical exemplar of the
"woman"* which is already clearly outlined in
the description of the "beginning" (cf. Gen.
3:15) and which proceeds from creation,
through sin and to the Redemption. In this
way there is a confirmation of the profound
union between what is human and what
constitutes the divine economy of salvation in
human history. The Bible convinces us of the
fact that one can have no hermeneutic of man,
or of what is "human," without appropriate
reference to what is "feminine." There is an
analogy in God's salvific economy: if we wish to

understand it fully in relation to the whole of human history, we cannot omit, in the perspective of our faith, the mystery of "woman": virgin-mother-spouse.

Mulieris Dignitatem, 22

The aim of any service in the Church, whether the service is apostolic, pastoral, priestly, or episcopal, is to keep up this dynamic link between the mystery of the Redemption and every man.

If we are aware of this task, then we seem to understand better what it means to say the Church is a mother and also what it means to say that the Church always, and particularly at our time, has need of a Mother. We owe a debt of special gratitude to the Fathers of the Second Vatican Council, who expressed this truth in the Constitution *Lumen Gentium* with the rich Mariological doctrine contained in it. Since Paul VI, inspired by that teaching, proclaimed the Mother of Christ "Mother of the Church," and that title has become known far and wide, may it be permitted to his unworthy successor to turn to Mary as Mother of the Church at the close of these reflections which it was opportune to make at the beginning of his papal service. Mary is Mother of the Church because, on account of the eternal

Father's ineffable choice and due to the Spirit of Love's special action, she gave human life to the Son of God, "for whom and by whom all things exist" and from whom the whole of the People of God receives the grace and dignity of election. Her Son explicitly extended his Mother's maternity in a way that could easily be understood by every soul and every heart by designating, when he was raised on the cross, his beloved disciple as her son. The Holy Spirit inspired her to remain in the Upper Room, after our Lord's Ascension, recollected with prayer and expectation, together with the Apostles, until the day of Pentecost, when the Church was to be born in visible form, coming forth from darkness. Later, all the generations of disciples, of those who confess and love Christ, like the Apostle John, spiritually took this Mother to their own homes, and she was thus included in the history of salvation and in the Church's mission from the very beginning, that is, from the moment of the Annunciation. Accordingly, we who form today's generation of disciples of Christ all wish to unite ourselves with her in a special way. We do so with all our attachment to our ancient tradition and also with full respect and love for the members of all the Christian communities.

Redemptor Hominis, 22

. . . So it is that we look at events near and far through the prism of these eternal words, uttered from the height of the cross. Through the prism of these words, a man was entrusted to the Mother of God as her Son. We all feel entrusted to Mary in that singular man. We therefore live with the consciousness of this trust in the Mother of God, with the whole nation, not only each on his own but also as a great community.

We feel embraced by these words: "There is your son." We feel that we are children, and we consider her our Mother. And let us extend this maternity of hers to all generations, to all occurrences, far or near. Let us read the signs of her motherhood in the development of those occurrences, which have never ceased to be full of hope for us, even with the difficulties involved. Such signs remain ours! They continue to remain ours because we have the Mother. Motherhood is the source of identity for each of us. Man's first right is to be descended directly from motherhood.

And so, this singular motherhood of Mary's — transmitted one time to the Evangelist and Apostle John, then extended to so many people and to entire nations, to our nation above all — gives us a particular sense of identity.

Insegnamenti, May, 3, 1982

As the Church contemplates Mary's motherhood, she discovers the meaning of her own motherhood and the way in which she is called to express it. At the same time, the Church's experience of motherhood leads to a most profound understanding of Mary's experience as the *incomparable model of how life should be welcomed and cared for.*
   Evangelium Vitae, 102

It is appropriate that Mary's song of praise, the *Magnificat*, should also find a place in our celebration: "My beginning proclaims the greatness of the Lord. . . . For he has looked upon his servant in her lowliness. . . . God who is mighty has done great things for me. . . . His mercy is from age to age . . . even as he promised our fathers, Abraham and his descendants forever" (Lk. 1:46-55).

Can we not suppose that these words, which reflect the fervor and exultation of the young Mother's heart, still ring true at the foot of the cross? That they still reveal her heart now that she finds herself in agony with her Son? Humanly speaking, it does not seem possible to us. However, within the fullness of divine truth, the words of the *Magnificat* actually *find their ultimate meaning* in the light of Christ's Paschal Mystery, from the cross through the Resurrection.

It is precisely in this Paschal Mystery that the "great things" — which God who is mighty has done for Mary — find their *perfect fulfillment,* not only for her, but for all of us and for all of humanity. It is precisely at the foot of the cross that the promise is fulfilled, which God once made to Abraham and to his descendants, the People of the Old Covenant. It is also at the foot of the cross that there is an overflow of *the mercy* shown to humanity from generation to generation by him whose name is holy.

Yes, at the foot of the cross, the "humility of the Lord's servant" — the one upon whom "God has looked" (cf. Lk. 1:48) — reaches its full measure together with the absolute humiliation of the Son of God. But from that same spot *the "blessing" of Mary by "all ages to come"* also begins.

Homily, Los Angeles, September 15, 1987

This Mother is Mary.
This Mother is also the Church.
Amen.

Address, Rome, February 2, 1980

Like the Church, Mary too had to live her motherhood amid suffering: "Behold, this child is set . . . for a sign that is spoken against (and a sword shall pierce your own soul also), so that the thoughts of many hearts may be revealed" (Lk. 2:34-35). The words which Simeon addresses to Mary at the very beginning of the Savior's earthly life sum up and prefigure the rejection of Jesus, and with him of Mary, a rejection which reached its culmination on Calvary. "Standing by the cross of Jesus" (Jn. 19:25), Mary shares in the gift which the Son makes of himself: she offers Jesus, gives him over, and begets him to the end for our sake. The "yes" spoken on the day of the Annunciation reaches full maturity on the day of the cross, when the time comes for Mary to receive and beget as her children all those who become disciples, pouring out upon them the saving love of her Son: "When Jesus saw his mother, and the disciple whom he loved standing near, he said to his mother, 'Woman, behold your son!' " (Jn. 19:26).

Evangelium Vitae, 103

Mary, who was present on the day of Pentecost at the beginning of the life of the Church with the Apostles, disciples, and pious women, always remains present in the Church, she, the first woman missionary, Mother and support of all those who proclaim the Gospel!

Address, Rome, October 12, 1979

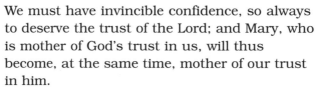

We must have invincible confidence, so always to deserve the trust of the Lord; and Mary, who is mother of God's trust in us, will thus become, at the same time, mother of our trust in him.

The pious invocation *"Mater mea, fiducia mea,"* so dear to all those who have been formed in this seminary, contains the deepest and fullest sense of our relationship with Mary, who is praised and venerated precisely by means of such regard of confidence, esteem, and hope. In fact, "the Father's eternal love, which has been manifested in the history of mankind through the Son . . . comes close to each of us through this Mother and thus takes on tokens that are more easily understood and accessible to each person. Consequently, Mary must be on all the ways for the Church's daily life" (*Redemptor Hominis*, 22).

Address, Lateran University, Rome,
February 16, 1980

As the Council proclaims: Mary became "a mother to us in the order of grace." This motherhood in the order of grace flows from her divine motherhood. Because she was, by the design of divine Providence, the Mother who nourished the divine Redeemer, Mary became "an associate of unique nobility, and the Lord's humble handmaid," who "cooperated by her obedience, faith, hope, and burning charity in the Savior's work of restoring supernatural life to souls." And "this *maternity of Mary in the order of grace* . . . will last without interruption until the eternal fulfillment of all the elect."

Redemptoris Mater, 22

Our Lady of the Bright Mountain, Mother of the Church! Once more I consecrate myself to you "in your maternal slavery of love": *Totus tuus!* — I am all yours! I consecrate to you the whole Church — everywhere and to the ends of the earth! I consecrate to you humanity; I consecrate to you all men and women, my brothers and sisters. All the peoples and the nations. I consecrate to you Europe and all the continents. I consecrate to you Rome and Poland, united through your servant, by a fresh bond of love.

Mother, accept us!
Mother, do not abandon us!
Mother, be our guide!

Homily, Jasna Góra, June 6, 1979

My last word is one of hope and prayer to
Mary, Mother of the Church. May she enable
all of us to fix our gaze constantly on her Son,
Jesus Christ, the great High Priest and chief
Shepherd of the Church of God.

Address, Rome, August 29, 1980

You are the future of the world, of the nation,
of the Church. "Tomorrow depends on you."
Accept with a sense of responsibility the simple
truth contained in this song of youth and ask
Christ, through his Mother, that you may be
able to face it.

Address, Kraków, June 8, 1979

Mother of the Church, grant that the Church
may enjoy freedom and peace in fulfilling her
saving mission and that to this end she may
become mature with *a new maturity* of faith
and inner unity. Help us to overcome
opposition and difficulties. Help us to

rediscover all the simplicity and dignity of the Christian vocation. Grant that there may be no lack of "laborers in the Lord's vineyard." Sanctify families. Watch over the souls of the young and the hearts of the children. Help us to overcome the great moral threats against the fundamental spheres of life and love. Obtain for us the grace to be continually renewed through all the beauty of witness given to the cross and resurrection of your Son.

How many problems, Mother, should I not present to you by name . . . ? I *entrust them all to you*, because you know them best and understand them.

Homily, Jasna Góra, June 4, 1979

7 / Mother of Mercy

O Mary,
Mother of Mercy,
watch over all people,
that the cross of Christ
may not be emptied
of its power,
that man may not stray from
the path of the good
or become blind to sin,
but may put his hope
ever more fully in God,
who is "rich in mercy"
(Eph. 2:4).
May he carry out
the good works prepared
by God beforehand
(cf. Eph. 2:10)
and so live completely
"for the praise
of his glory"
(Eph. 1:12).

Veritatis Splendor, 120

Dear brothers, at the beginning of my ministry I entrust all of you to the Mother of Christ, who in a special way is our Mother: the Mother of the Priests. In fact, the beloved disciple, who, as one of the Twelve, had heard in the Upper Room the words "Do this in memory of me," was given by Christ on the cross to his Mother, with the words "Behold your son." The man who on Holy Thursday received the power to celebrate the Eucharist was, by these words of the dying Redeemer, given to his Mother as her "son." All of us, therefore, who receive the same power through priestly ordination have in a certain sense a prior right to see her as our Mother. And so I desire that all of you, together with me, should find in Mary the mother of the priesthood which we have received from Christ. I also desire that you should entrust your priesthood to her in a special way. Allow me to do it myself, entrusting to the Mother of Christ each one of you — without any exception — in a solemn and at the same time simple and humble way. And I ask each of you, dear brothers, to do it yourselves, in the way dictated to you in your heart, especially by your love for Christ the Priest, and also by your own weaknesses, which go hand in hand with your desire for service and holiness. I ask you to do this.

"To All the Bishops of the Church," 11

She carries the Child in her arms. He, even in her hands, is the Light of our souls, the Light that illumines the darkness of knowledge and of human existence, of the intellect and the heart.

The thoughts of so many hearts are revealed when her mother's hands carry this great divine Light, when they bring it closer to man.

Hail, you who became Mother of our Light at the cost of the great sacrifice of your Son, at the cost of the motherly sacrifice of your heart!

And, finally, allow me, today, on the day after my return from Mexico, to thank you, O Lady of Guadalupe, for this Light which your Son is for the sons and daughters of that country and also of the whole of Latin America.

Address, Rome, February 2, 1979

The titles which we attribute to the Mother of God speak of her principally, however, as the Mother of the crucified and risen One; as *the One who, having obtained mercy in an exceptional way,* in an equally exceptional way *"merits" that mercy* throughout her earthly life and, particularly, at the foot of the cross of her Son; and finally as the one who, through her hidden and at the same time incomparable sharing in the messianic mission of her Son, was called in a special way to bring close to people that love which he had come to reveal: the love that finds its most concrete expression *vis-à-vis* the suffering, the poor, those deprived of their own freedom, the blind, the oppressed, and sinners, just as Christ spoke of them in the words of the prophecy of Isaiah, first in the synagogue at Nazareth and then in response to the question of the messengers of John the Baptist.

It was precisely the "merciful" love, which is manifested above all in contact with moral and physical evil, that the heart of her who was the Mother of the crucified and risen One shared in singularly and exceptionally — that Mary shared in. In her and through her, this love continues to be revealed in the history of the Church and of humanity. This revelation is especially fruitful because in the Mother of God it is based upon the unique fact of her maternal heart, on her particular sensitivity, on her particular fitness to reach all those *who most easily accept the merciful love of a mother.* This is one of the great life-giving mysteries of the Incarnation.

Dives in Misericordia, 9

To Mary who is the Mother of divine grace I entrust priestly and religious vocations. May the new spring of vocations, their new increase throughout the Church, become a particular proof of her motherly presence in the mystery of Christ, in our times, and in the mystery of his Church all over the earth. Mary alone is a living incarnation to God, to Christ, to his salvific action, which must find its adequate expression in every priestly and religious vocation. Mary is the fullest expression of perfect faithfulness to the Holy Spirit and to his action in the soul; she is the expression of the faithfulness which means persevering cooperation in the grace of vocation.

Audience, Rome, May 2, 1979

To all of you gathered here, I desire to wish the same joy announced by Isaiah and lived intensely by Mary: the joy of God's salvific gift which passes through your personal vocation, the unrepeatable expression of his fatherly confidence in you. To you who are already aware and certain of your call, and of the consequent responsible commitment, I wish the joy of happy possession of the divine gift and sweet experience of it; while to those, already in the seminary or still outside it, who are in trusting quest of their own way, I wish the happiness of listening serenely to God's voice and of an explorative path, carried out in the certainty that the Lord fills the hungry with good things and helps his servants, because of his mercy (cf. Lk. 1:53-54).

Address, Lateran University, Rome, February 16, 1980

Remember that the power of Christ's Paschal Mystery will supply for your weakness and fill your hearts with love. And the Mother of Jesus will never abandon you.

Dear young people: this is a special honor for you and for the whole Christian community. It is an hour of commitment and responsibility, an hour of generosity and joy! Will you not open wide your hearts to Christ's call and mine: "Come, follow me"? And may the entire Church . . . be filled with a renewed sense of mission and with fresh vigor and strength: in the name of the Father, and of the Son, and of the Holy Spirit. Amen.

Address to the Youth of Australia, April 1980

With renewed pastoral love and zeal let us proclaim his saving Word to the world. Relying on the assistance of Mary, Mother of the Incarnate Word, let us together commend our people and our ministry to him who alone has "the words of eternal life" (Jn. 6:68).
Address, Rome, June 7, 1980

Mary is also the one who obtained mercy in a particular and exceptional way, as no other person has. At the same time, still in an exceptional way, she made possible with the sacrifice of her heart her own sharing in revealing God's mercy. This sacrifice is intimately linked with the cross of her Son, at the foot of which she was to stand on Calvary. Her sacrifice is a unique sharing in the revelation of mercy, that is, a sharing in the absolute fidelity of God to his own love, to the Covenant that he willed from eternity and that he entered into in time with man, with the people, with humanity; it is a sharing in the revelation that was definitively fulfilled through the cross. *No one has experienced, to the same degree as the Mother of the crucified One,* the mystery of the cross, the overwhelming encounter of divine transcendent justice with

love: that "kiss" given by mercy to justice. No
one has received into his heart, as much as
Mary did, that mystery, that truly divine
dimension of the Redemption effected on
Calvary by means of the death of the Son,
together with the sacrifice of her maternal
heart, together with her definitive *"fiat."*

Mary, then, is the one who *has the deepest
knowledge of the mystery of God's mercy.* She
knows its price, she knows how great it is. In
this sense, we call her the *Mother of mercy,* our
Lady of mercy, or Mother of divine mercy; In
each one of these titles there is a deep
theological meaning, for they express the
special preparation of her soul, of her whole
personality, so that she was able to perceive,
through the complex events, first of Israel,
then of every individual and of the whole of
humanity, the mercy of which "from generation
to generation" people become sharers
according to the eternal design of the most
holy Trinity.

Divus In Misericordia, 9

Let our service, dear brothers and sisters,
which has the supreme aim of making men
convinced of the heavenly Father's love, be
entrusted entirely to the Mother of God and
our Mother, so greatly loved and celebrated by

our saint, who has expressions of extraordinary tenderness for her, admirably exalting her in her mission as bestower of grace.

In this perspective of hope and confidence, I call down upon all of you the fullness of heavenly gifts and I gladly impart my affectionate blessing to you and to all your dear ones.

Address, Abruzzi, Italy, August 30, 1980

The missionaries who came to proclaim the Gospel began their missionary service with an act of consecration to the Mother of Christ.

They addressed her as follows:

"Here we are, among those who are our brothers and our sisters, and whom your Son, O Virgin Mary, loved to the end. Out of love, he offered his life for them on the cross; out of love, he remains in the Eucharist to be the nourishment of souls; out of love, he founded the Church to be the unshakable community in which salvation is found. All this is still unknown to these brothers and these sisters among whom we arrive; they do not know yet the Good News of the Gospel. But we believe deeply that their hearts and their consciences are prepared to accept the Gospel of salvation

thanks to the sacrifice of Christ, and also to
your motherly intercession and meditation."

Homily, Kinshasa, Zaire, May 2, 1980

May your families, in joy as well as in
hardship, be a reflection of God's love! May the
Virgin Mother, contemplated and prayed to
within each Christian family, lead you along
the way to her Son and open you up to the
light and power of the Holy Spirit, in peace! I
willingly bless all the members of your families,
husbands and wives, children and young
people, grandparents. And I also bless the
couples who are dear to you and who are
relying on your witness.

Address, Rome, November 8, 1980

In these times of ours, in which the true
beauty of conjugal love is threatened in so
many ways — threatened together with the
dignity of fatherhood and motherhood — have
courage! Have inflexible courage to look for it,
to bear witness to it to each other, and to the
world. Be apostles of the dignity of parenthood.
Be apostles of beautiful love. So I commend
you, dear brothers and sisters, to the Mother of
God — to her whom the Church professed as

Theotokos fifteen hundred and fifty years ago at the Council of Ephesus, and whom we recall this year, too.

Address, Rome, May 3, 1981

Evangelization "is the great ministry or service that the Church carries out for the world and for men, the Good News that the kingdom of justice and peace reaches men in Jesus Christ" (Puebla Document, 679). Hence the Church, if she wishes to be really the bearer of the message of the Son of God, must proclaim, live, and bear witness to the Gospel faithfully and consistently. In the evangelizing history of the Church, the Virgin Mary has occupied and continues to occupy a singularly unique place. It has rightly been said: "to Christ through Mary."

Address, Mendoza, Argentina, October 12, 1980

8 / Mother of the Redeemer

You who are *the first among the redeemed*, help us, men and women of the twentieth century moving toward its end and, at the same time, are people of the second millennium after Christ. Help us to find once more our part in the mystery of the Redemption. Help us to understand more profoundly the divine dimension and, at the same time, the human dimensions of that mystery. Help us to draw more fully on its inexhaustible resources. Help us — redeemed by the most precious blood of Christ. All this we ask of you in the solemnity of today, O clement, O pious, O sweet Virgin Mary. Amen.

Insegnamenti, December 8, 1982

Since "the Church is in Christ as a sacrament . . . of intimate union with God and of the unity of the whole human race" (*Lumen Gentium*, 1), the special presence of the Mother of God in the mystery of the Church makes us think *of the exceptional link between this "woman" and the whole human family*. It is a question here of every man and woman, all the sons and daughters of the human race, in whom from generation to generation a *fundamental inheritance* is realized, the inheritance that belongs to all humanity and that is linked with the mystery of the biblical "beginning": "God created man in his own image, in the image of God he created him; male and female he created them" (Gen. 1:27).

Mulieris Dignitatem, 2

Has man ever been able to attain to anything more exalted? Has he ever been able to experience about himself anything more profound? Has man been able through any achievement of his being man — through his intellect, the greatness of his mind, or through heroic deeds — to be lifted up to a higher state than has been given him in this "fruit of the womb" of Mary. . . ?

Address, Altotting, Germany, November 18, 1980

In the Byzantine liturgy, in all the hours of the Divine Office, praise of the Mother is linked with praise of her Son and with the praise which, through the Son, is offered up to the Father in the Holy Spirit. In the Anaphora or Eucharistic Prayer of St. John Chrysostom, immediately after the epiclesis the assembled community sings in honor of the Mother of God: "It is truly just to proclaim you blessed, O Mother of God, who are most blessed, all pure and Mother of our God. We magnify you who are more honorable than the Cherubim and incomparably more glorious than the Seraphim. You who, without losing your virginity, gave birth to the Word of God. You who are truly the Mother of God."

These praises, which in every celebration of the Eucharistic Liturgy are offered to Mary, have molded the faith, piety, and prayer of the faithful. In the course of the centuries they have permeated their whole spiritual outlook, fostering in them a profound devotion to the "All-Holy Mother of God."

Redemptoris Mater, 32

The Mother of Christ calls us, invites us to join with the Church of the living God in the consecration of the world, in this act of confiding by which the world, mankind as a whole, the nations, and each individual person are presented to the eternal Father with the power of the Redemption won by Christ. They are offered in the heart of the Redeemer which was pierced on the cross.

Address, Fátima, May 13, 1982

This presence of Mary finds different expressions in our day, just as it did throughout the Church's history. It also has a wide field of action. Through the faith and piety of individual believers; through the traditions of Christian families or "domestic churches," of parish and missionary communities, religious institutes and dioceses; through the radiance and attraction of the great shrines where not only individuals or local groups but sometimes whole nations and societies, even whole continents, seek to meet the Mother of the Lord, the one who is blessed because she believed as the first among believers and therefore became the Mother of Emmanuel.

Redemptoris Mater, 28

I entrust this responsibility of the whole Church to the maternal intercession of Mary, Mother of the Redeemer. She, the mother of fairest love, will be for Christians on the way to the Great Jubilee of the third millennium the star which safely guides their steps to the Lord. May the unassuming young woman of Nazareth, who two thousand years ago offered to the world the Incarnate Word, lead the men and women of the new millennium toward the one who is "the true light that enlightens every man" (Jn. 1:9).

With these sentiments I impart to all my blessing.

Tertio Millennio Adveniente, 59

The Second Vatican Council prepares us for this by presenting in its teaching *the Mother of God in the mystery of Christ and the Church.* If it is true, as the Council itself proclaims, that "only in the mystery of the Incarnate Word does the mystery of man take on light," then this principle must be applied in a very particular way to that exceptional "daughter of the human race," that extraordinary "woman" who became the Mother of Christ. Only *in the mystery of Christ* is *her mystery fully made clear.* Thus has the Church sought to interpret it from the very beginning: the mystery of the Incarnation has enabled her to penetrate and to make ever clearer the mystery of the Mother of the Incarnate Word. The Council of Ephesus (431) was of decisive importance in clarifying this, for during that Council, to the great joy of Christians, the truth of the divine motherhood of Mary was solemnly confirmed as a truth of the Church's faith. Mary *is the Mother of God* (i.e., *Theotokos*), since by the power of the Holy Spirit she conceived in her virginal womb and brought into the world Jesus Christ, the Son of God, who is one being with the Father. "The Son of God . . . born of the Virgin Mary . . . has truly been made one of us," has been made man. Thus, through the mystery of Christ, on the horizon of the Church's faith there shines in its fullness the mystery of his Mother. In turn, the dogma of the divine motherhood of Mary was for the Council of Ephesus and is for the Church like a seal upon the dogma of the Incarnation, in which the Word truly assumes human nature into the unity of his person, without canceling out that nature.

Redemptoris Mater, 4

Mary, the Mother of the Redeemer, constantly remained beside Christ in his journey toward the human family and in its midst, and she goes before the Church on the pilgrimage of faith. May her maternal intercession accompany humanity toward the next millennium, in fidelity to him who "is the same yesterday and today and for ever" (cf. Heb. 13:8), Jesus Christ our Lord, in whose name I cordially impart my blessing to all.

Centesimus Annus, 62

For if we feel a special need, in this difficult and responsible phase of the history of the Church and of mankind, to turn to Christ, who is Lord of the Church and Lord of man's history on account of the mystery of the Redemption, we believe that nobody else can bring us as Mary can into the divine and human dimension of this mystery. Nobody has been brought into it by God himself as Mary has. It is in this that the exceptional character of the grace of the divine motherhood consists. Not only is the dignity of this motherhood unique and unrepeatable in the history of the human race, but Mary's participation, due to this maternity, in God's plan for man's salvation through the mystery of the Redemption is also unique in profundity and range of action.

We can say that the mystery of the Redemption took shape beneath the heart of the Virgin of Nazareth when she pronounced her *"fiat."* From then on, under the special influence of the Holy Spirit, this heart, the heart of both a virgin and a mother, has always followed the work of her Son and has gone out to all those whom Christ has embraced and continues to embrace with inexhaustible love. For that reason her heart must also have the inexhaustibility of a mother. The special characteristic of the motherly love that the

Mother of God inserts in the mystery of the Redemption and the life of the Church finds expression in its exceptional closeness to man and all that happens to him. It is in this that the mystery of the Mother consists. The Church, which looks to her with altogether special love and hope, wishes to make this mystery her own in an ever deeper manner. For in this the Church also recognizes the way for her daily life, which is each person.

The Father's eternal love, which has been manifested in the history of mankind through the Son whom the Father gave, "that whoever believes in him should not perish but have eternal life," comes close to each of us through this Mother and thus takes on tokens that are of more easy understanding and access by each person. Consequently, Mary must be on all the ways for the Church's daily life. Through her maternal presence the Church acquires certainty that she is living the life of her Master and Lord and that she is living the mystery of Redemption in all its life-giving profundity and fullness. Likewise the Church, which has struck root in many varied fields of the life of the whole of present-day humanity, also acquires the certainty and, one could say, the experience of being close to man, to each person, of being each person's Church, the Church of the People of God.

Redemptor Hominis, 22

The particular union of the *Theotokos* with God — which fulfills in the most eminent manner the supernatural predestination to union with the Father which is granted to every human being (*filii in Filio*) — is a pure grace and, as such, *a gift of the Spirit*. At the same time, however, through her response of faith Mary exercises her free will and thus fully shares with her personal and feminine "I" in the event of the Incarnation. With her "*fiat*," Mary becomes the *authentic subject* of that union with God which was realized in the mystery of the Incarnation of the Word, who is of one substance with the Father. All of God's action in human history at all times respects the free will of the human "I." And such was the case with the Annunciation at Nazareth.

Mulieris Dignitatem, 4

In the mystery of Christ she is *present* even "before the creation of the world," as the one whom the Father "has chosen" as *Mother* of his Son in the Incarnation. And, what is more, together with the Father, the Son has chosen her, entrusting her eternally to the Spirit of holiness. In an entirely special and exceptional way Mary is united to Christ, and similarly she *is eternally loved in this "beloved Son,"* this

Son who is of one being with the Father, in whom is concentrated all the "glory of grace." At the same time, she is and remains perfectly open to this "gift from above" (cf. Jas. 1:17). As the Council teaches, Mary "stands out among the poor and humble of the Lord, who confidentially await and receive salvation from him."

If the greeting and the name "full of grace" say all this, in the context of the angel's announcement they refer first of all *to the election of Mary as Mother of the Son of God.* But at the same time the "fullness of grace" indicates all the supernatural munificence from which Mary benefits by being chosen and destined to be the Mother of Christ. If this election is fundamental for the accomplishment of God's salvific designs for humanity, and if the eternal choice in Christ and the vocation to the dignity of adopted children is the destiny of everyone, then the election of Mary is wholly exceptional and unique. Hence also the singularity and uniqueness of her place in the mystery of Christ.

Redemptoris Mater, 8-9

Motherhood has been introduced into the order of the Covenant that God made with humanity in Jesus Christ. Each and every time that *motherhood* is repeated in human history, it is always *related to the Covenant* which God established with the human race through the motherhood of the Mother of God.

Mulieris Dignitatem, 19

. . . [Y]ou love the Mother of Jesus. I know that the Madonna of Grace is especially dear to you; her image is filially preserved and venerated in your beautiful cathedral. I am highly pleased, and I urge you to persevere in this devotion of yours that, if rightly understood and lived, will surely lead to the constantly increasing penetration of the mystery of Christ, our only Savior. The heart of his Mother is great and tender enough to pour forth her own love also on each one of us, needful as we are of her protection every day. Therefore, let us invoke her with full trust.

Homily, Velletri, Italy, September 7, 1980

We are all equally indebted to our Redeemer. We should all listen together to that Spirit of truth and of love whom he has promised to the Church and who is operative in her. In the name of this truth and of this love, in the name of the crucified Christ and of his Mother, I ask you, and beg you: Let us abandon all opposition and division, and let us all unite in this great mission of salvation which is the price and at the same time the fruit of our redemption.

Dominicae Cenae, 13

We have every right to believe that our generation, too, was included in the words of the Mother of God when she glorified that mercy shared in "from generation to generation" by those who allow themselves to be guided by the fear of God. The words of Mary's *Magnificat* have a prophetic content that concerns not only the past of Israel but also the whole future of the People of God on earth. In fact, all of us now living on earth are *the generation* that is aware of the approach of the third millennium and that profoundly *feels the change* that is occurring in history.

Dives in Misericordia, 10

So to her, the Mother of the Redeemer and the Mother of our hope, I entrust you all: priests, sisters, fathers and mothers of families, children, the young, the sick, those who live in loneliness, the abandoned, the aged, the suffering. Those who work in the fields, in factories, in universities, in schools, in offices.

All together and each one individually, you who are present here and all those united with us spiritually. I entrust to her your present and your future, your faith, hope, and charity. Your work, joys, concerns, and worries. I entrust to her in a special way the young generation and their future.

Address, Curitiba, Brazil, July 5, 1980

The Sunday within the octave of Christmas, that is, the present Sunday, unites in the liturgy the solemn memory of the Holy Family of Jesus, Mary, and Joseph. The birth of a child always gives rise to a family. The birth of Jesus in Bethlehem gave rise to this unique and exceptional family in the history of mankind. In this family there came into the world, grew, and was brought up the Son of God, conceived and born of the Virgin Mother, and at the same time entrusted, from the beginning, to the truly fatherly care of Joseph. The latter — a carpenter of Nazareth, who *vis-à-vis* Jewish law was Mary's husband, and *vis-à-vis* the Holy Spirit was her worthy spouse and the guardian — was really, in a fatherly way, of the maternal mystery of his bride.

Homily, Rome, December 31, 1978

9 / Mystical Rose

Let us continue on our way, therefore, with renewed energy. The Blessed Virgin indicates the way to us. Like the bright morning star, she shines before the eyes of our faith "as a sign of sure hope and solace, until the day of the Lord shall come" (*Lumen Gentium*, 68). Pilgrims in this "vale of tears," we sigh to her: "Show us after this our exile, Jesus, the blessed fruit of your womb, O clement, O pious, O sweet Virgin Mary!"

Address, Lourdes, February 11, 1980

Take from the "Mother of mercy" and "Consolation of the afflicted" an example and inspiration at every moment. She will guide you to her Son and will teach you the value of every soul.

Address, Rome, May 23, 1980

When Elizabeth greeted her young kinswoman coming from Nazareth, Mary replied with the *Magnificat*. In her greeting, Elizabeth first called Mary "blessed" because of "the fruit of her womb," and then she called her "blessed"

because of her faith (cf. Lk. 1:42, 45). These two blessings referred directly to the Annunciation. Now, at the Visitation, when Elizabeth's greeting bears witness to that culminating moment, Mary's faith acquires a new consciousness and a new expression. That which remained hidden in the depths of the "obedience of faith" at the Annunciation can now be said to spring forth like a clear and life-giving flame of the spirit. The words used by Mary on the threshold of Elizabeth's house are *an inspired profession of her faith,* in which *her response to the revealed word* is expressed with the religious and poetical exultation of her whole being toward God. In these sublime words, which are simultaneously very simple and wholly inspired by the sacred texts of the people of Israel, Mary's personal experience, the ecstasy of her heart, shines forth. In them shines a ray of the mystery of God, the glory of his ineffable holiness, the eternal *love which, as an irrevocable gift, enters into human history.*

Redemptoris Mator, 36

The history of "fairest love" begins at the Annunciation, in those wondrous words which the angel spoke to Mary, called to become the Mother of the Son of God. With Mary's "yes," the One who is "God from God and Light from

Light" becomes a son of man. Mary is his Mother, while continuing to be the Virgin who "knows not man" (cf. Lk. 1:34). As Mother and Virgin, Mary becomes the *Mother of fairest love*. This truth is already revealed in the words of the Archangel Gabriel, but its full significance will gradually become clearer and more evident as Mary follows her Son in the pilgrimage of faith.

Letter to Families, February 22, 1994

. . . [E]ven though it is not possible to establish an exact *chronological point* for identifying the date of Mary's birth, the Church has constantly been aware that *Mary appeared* on the horizon of *salvation history before Christ.* It is a fact that when "the fullness of time" was definitively drawing near — the saving advent of Emmanuel — she who was from eternity destined to be his Mother already existed on earth. The fact that she "preceded" the coming of Christ is reflected every year *in the liturgy of Advent.* Therefore, if to that ancient historical expectation of the Savior we compare these years which are bringing us closer to the end of the second millennium after Christ and to the beginning of the third, it becomes fully comprehensible that in this present period we wish to turn in a special way to her, the one who in the "night" of the Advent expectation began to shine like a true "Morning Star" (*Stella Matutina*). For just as this star, together with the "dawn," precedes the rising of the sun, so Mary from the time of her Immaculate Conception preceded the coming of the Savior, the rising of the "Sun of Justice" in the history of the human race. . . . With good reason, then, at the end of this millennium, we Christians who know that the providential plan of the most holy Trinity is *the central reality of Revelation and of faith* feel the need to emphasize the unique presence of the Mother of Christ in history, especially during these last years leading up to the year 2000.

Redemptoris Mater, 3

When the Virgin was proclaimed blessed together with "the fruit of your womb" and proclaimed blessed for having believed, she replied, "Yes," but then *changed the person whom she addressed,* for she began to speak to the Lord, and raised a marvelous song of praise to him in her lowliness of a servant. The *Magnificat* is the real Song of Songs of the New Testament, resounding on our lips daily, brethren. Let us try to intone it with particular fervor . . . so that, in spiritual union with Mary, we may repeat it . . . almost syllable by syllable, and so learn from her how and why we, too, ought to bless the Lord.

She teaches us that God alone is great and therefore ought to be called magnificent by us. He alone saves us; therefore our spirits should exult in him. He bows toward us with his mercy and raises us to him through his power. Grand, indeed, and lofty is the lesson of the *Magnificat*. Each of us can and should make it his or her own, in all conditions of life, to attain comfort and serenity — beyond the gifts of grace and light — even in trials brought by tribulations and in the sufferings of the body itself.

Insegnamenti, **February 14, 1982**

From the time when Jesus, dying on the cross, said to John: "Behold your mother"; from the time when "the disciple took her to his own home," the mystery of the spiritual motherhood of Mary has been actualized boundlessly in history. Motherhood means sharing in the life of the child. Since Mary is the mother of us all, her care for the life of man is universal. The care of a mother embraces her child totally. Mary's motherhood has its beginning in her motherly care for Christ. In Christ, at the foot of the cross, she accepted John, and in John she accepted all of us totally. Mary embraces us all with special solicitude in the Holy Spirit.

For as we profess in our Creed, he is "the giver of life." It is he who gives the fullness of life, open toward eternity.

Mary's spiritual motherhood is therefore a sharing in the power of the Holy Spirit, of "the giver of life." It is the humble service of her who says of herself: "Behold, I am the handmaid of the Lord" (Lk. 1:38).

In the light of the mystery of Mary's spiritual motherhood, let us seek to understand the extraordinary message, which began on May 13, 1917, to resound throughout the world from Fátima, continuing for five months until October 13 of the same year.

Address, Fátima, May 13, 1982

Mary, who conceived the Incarnate Word by the power of the Holy Spirit and then in the whole of her life allowed herself to be guided by his interior activity . . . as the woman who was docile to the voice of the Spirit, a woman of silence and attentiveness, a woman of hope who, like Abraham, accepted God's will "hoping against hope" (cf. Rom 4:18). Mary gave full expression to the longing of the poor of Yahweh and is a radiant model for those who entrust themselves with all their hearts to the promises of God.

Tertio Millennio Adveniente, 48

Mary . . . helps the Church to *realize* that life is always at the center of a great struggle between good and evil, between light and darkness. The dragon wishes to devour "the child brought forth" (cf. Rev. 12:4), a figure of Christ, whom Mary brought forth "in the fullness of time" (Gal. 4:4) and whom the Church must unceasingly offer to people in every age. But in a way that child is also a figure of every person, every child, especially every helpless baby whose life is threatened, because as the Council reminds us — "by his Incarnation the Son of God has united himself in some fashion with every person."

Evangelium Vitae, 104

May Mary most holy, who was totally sanctified by the Holy Spirit, make you always feel the joy of the "soul's sweet Guest," make you always open to his inspirations, and keep you always burning with enthusiasm to be handmaids of infinite and merciful Love!

Address, Rome, October 23, 1982

Always know how to gather and preserve the first roots of your being, which are the will of the Father, the grace of Christ, the power of the Spirit — the three most holy Persons, welcomed and working in the most pure heart of the Mother of God from the very first moment of her conception. May you also be, like the Child Mary, the blessed place, the temple of welcome of this infinite Mystery, so that shattered and disheartened humanity might find consolation, light, and rest in this "place."

Address, Rome, October 23, 1982

I wish in particular to bring the youth of the whole world and of the whole Church closer to her, to Mary, who is the Mother of fair love. She bears within her an indestructible sign of youth and beauty which never pass. I wish and pray that the young will approach her, have confidence in her, and entrust to her the life that is before them; that they will love her with a simple and warm love of the heart.

Audience, Rome, May 2, 1979

"I will greatly rejoice in the Lord; my soul shall exult in my God" (Is. 61:10).

The joy of the soul in God, manifested by Isaiah in these words, at once turns our thoughts to Mary, who expressed her joy

particularly in the song of the *Magnificat.*
Mary's joy was the joy of grace, of the gift
received — that is, the vocation to be called by
God to a mission which certainly represents
the peak of woman's dignity and aspiration.
Thanks to her, there was to be realized the
great, unfathomable mystery, which the people
of Israel, interpreting the desire and the
expectation of the whole of mankind, kept in
its deepest and most living religious tradition:
the presence of "Emmanuel," that is, of God
with us.

Mary's joy was, therefore, joy for the trust
that God had shown in her by entrusting
himself to her in the Person of his only Son.
Bearing in her womb the Word Incarnate, and
giving him to the world, she became the
extraordinary depository of God's trust in man,
so that Mary is rightly honored as the Mother
of Divine Confidence.

Address, Rome, February 16, 1980

May the Virgin Mary always sustain you on the
way, and may she introduce you more and
more every day to intimacy with the Lord! With
my affectionate apostolic blessing.

Homily, Kinshasa, Zaire, May 4, 1980

. . . [W]ith the prayer of the *Angelus* or *Regina Caeli*, I address to the Church and to the world in numerous circumstances, taking advantage of the riches of tradition, of the Marian piety of the individual local Churches, and of the various nations, which have blossomed in numberless gracious and moving forms of honor of the Blessed Virgin. Here, too, the fundamental doctrinal inspiration comes from the Council, from the Constitution *Lumen Gentium*, which . . . gave a global synthesis, sober in its extraordinary richness, of Marian theology, and called upon all believers to set out with greater commitment along the royal way of true Marian piety, which leads to Christ.

Address, Rome, Feast of Sts. Peter and Paul, 1980

Mary brings to the Upper Room at Pentecost the "new motherhood" which became her "part" at the foot of the cross. This motherhood is to remain in her, and at the same time it is to be transferred from her as a "model" to the whole Church, which will be revealed to the world on the day of the descent of the Holy Spirit, the Paraclete. All those gathered in the Upper Room are aware that, from the moment of

Christ's return to the Father, their life is hid with him in God. Mary lives in this awareness more than anyone else.

__Marian Year Letter to All Consecrated Persons__, **1988**

10 / Our Lady of the Rosary

Dear brothers and sisters: we are confident that Mary, the Mother of God and the Mother of life, will give us her help so that our way of living will always reflect our admiration and gratitude for God's gift of love that is life. We know that she will help us to use every day that is given to us as an opportunity to defend the life of the unborn and to render more human the lives of all our fellow human beings, wherever they may be.

And through the intercession of Our Lady of the Rosary, whose feast we celebrate today, may we come one day to the fullness of eternal life in Christ Jesus our Lord. Amen.

Homily, Capitol Mall, Washington, D.C., October 7, 1979

You show your devotion to Mary by celebrating her feasts, by daily prayer in her honor and especially the rosary, and by imitating her life. May that devotion grow stronger every day.

Address, Manila, February 17, 1981

The rosary is the prayer through which, by repeating the angel's greeting to Mary, we try to draw considerations of our own on the mysteries of Redemption from the Blessed Virgin's meditation. Her reflection began at the moment of the Annunciation and continues in the glory of the Assumption.

L'Osservatore Romano, October 1983

Mary enters the house of her relative, she greets Elizabeth, and hears her words of greeting. These words are familiar to us. We repeat them innumerable times, especially when we meditate on the mysteries of the rosary: "*Blessed are you among women*, and blessed is the fruit of your womb" (Lk. 1:42). That is how the wife of Zachary greets Mary.

Address, Altotting, Germany, November 18, 1980

The call to repentance is a motherly one, and at the same time it is strong and decisive. The love that "rejoices in the truth" (cf. 1 Cor. 13:6) is capable of being clear-cut and firm. The call to repentance is linked, as always, with a call to prayer. In harmony with the tradition of many centuries, the Lady of the message indicates the *rosary*, which can rightly be defined as "Mary's prayer": the prayer in which she feels particularly united with us. She herself prays with us. The rosary prayer embraces the problems of the Church, of the See of St. Peter, the problems of the whole world. In it we also remember sinners, that they may be converted and saved. . . .

Address, Fátima, May 13, 1982

. . . It was "thanks to the Lord that I was not assassinated." I said that the first time on the occasion of the feast of the Virgin of the Rosary. I say it again now, at Fátima, which speaks so much to us about the rosary — of recitation of the third part of the rosary — as the little shepherds were reciting. The rosary, its third part — is and ever shall be a prayer of thanksgiving, of love and of confident entreaty, the prayer of the Mother of the Church!

I have come on pilgrimage to Fátima, like most of you, dear pilgrims, with the rosary beads in my hand, the name of Mary on my lips and the song of the mercy of God in my heart.

Insegnamenti, **May 12, 1982**

Turn to Mary most holy, your heavenly Mother; pray to her with fervor, especially by means of the rosary; invoke her daily, in order to be authentic imitators of Christ in our day.

Address, Nuaro, Italy, October 19, 1985

The Church's veneration for the Madonna — a veneration that surpasses the cult of any other saint and takes the name of "hyperdulia" — invests the whole liturgical year. March 25 is the day on which the moment of the Annunciation, that is, the Incarnation of the eternal Word in the Virgin's pure womb, is recalled. From that day up to December 25, it can be said that the Church discreetly but with deep awareness, walks with Mary, living with her the expectancy of every mother: expectancy of the birth, expectancy of Christmas. And at the same time, during this period, Mary "walks" with the Church. Her motherly expectancy is inscribed, in a quiet but very real way, in the life of the Church throughout the year. What happened between Nazareth, Ain Karim, and Bethlehem is the subject of the liturgy of the Church, of its prayer — especially the prayer of the rosary — and its contemplation.

Address, Rome, January 10, 1979

But let us pray with constancy and confidence to the Blessed Virgin, the Queen of Missions, that she make the faithful feel ever more deeply concerned for evangelization and responsibility for the proclamation of the Gospel. Let us pray to her in particular with the recitation of the holy rosary, to reach in this way, and to help those who are laboring amid difficulties and hardships, to make Jesus known and loved!

Address, Rome, October 21, 1979

And now for a fatherly and affectionate thought for you, dear young people.

I will take the opportunity of the feast of the Blessed Virgin, celebrated yesterday, but which in a way extends throughout the whole month of October. The holy rosary introduces us into the very heart of faith. With our thought fixed on it, we greet repeatedly, joyfully, the holy Mother of God; declare blessed the Son, the sweet fruit of her womb; and invoke her motherly protection in life and in death.

The holy rosary, with its alternating verses of joy and sorrow, as well as hope and resurrection, may be of use to you, too, dear sick people who are present, or who have remained at home. It shows, through the vicissitudes of the Son of God and of the Virgin, how constant in human life is the alteration of good and evil, calm and storms, joyful days and sad ones. Sorrow weighs on human nature, created for joy; but it is also a regenerating and sanctifying element, as we can see very well in the life of Christ and his Mother.

Address, Rome, October 8, 1980

This gives rise to the necessity of a continual renewal in a special union with Mary, Mother of Christ and Mother of the Church. "To her" — I said before Christmas — "I entrusted the beginning of my pontificate, to her I have brought, in the course of the year, the expression of my filial piety, which I learned from my parents. Mary has been the star of my way, in her most famous or most silent sanctuaries" (*Insegnamenti*, II, 2, 1979, p. 1497). In these six months there have been added a list of those places, so dear to my heart, other sweet names: the Consolata and the "Great Mother," in Turin; Our Lady of Zaire, in Kinshasa; Our Lady of the Rosary, in Kisangani; Notre Dame, in Paris; and in the Ivory Coast I laid the first stone of the Church of "Our Lady of Africa."

Address, Rome, Feast of Sts. Peter and Paul, 1980

11 / Our Lady of Sorrows

But there is another image of the Mother with the Son in her arms: the "Pietà," Mary holding Jesus taken down from the cross. With Jesus, who expired before her eyes . . . and, after death, he returned to those arms in which at Bethlehem he was offered as Savior of the world.

I would therefore join our prayer of peace with this twofold image: "Mother, you who know what it is to hold the corpse of your Son in your arms, . . . spare all mothers the death of their sons, torments, slavery, the destructions of war, persecutions, concentration camps, prisons! Preserve the joy of birth to them, of nourishment, of development of man and of his life.

"In the name . . . of the birth of the Lord, implore peace together with us, with all the beauty and majesty of your motherhood, which the Church exalts and the world admires. We beg you: be with us at every moment. Make this New Year a year of peace by virtue of the birth and death of your Son! Amen."

Insegnamenti, January 1, 1979

The days which follow the birth of Jesus are also feast days: so *eight days afterwards,* according to the Old Testament tradition, the Child was given a name: he was called Jesus. *After forty days,* we commemorate his presentation at the Temple, like every other firstborn son of Israel. On that occasion, an extraordinary meeting took place: Mary, when she arrived at the Temple with the Child, was met by the old man Simeon, who took the Baby Jesus in his arms and spoke these prophetic words: "Lord, now let your servant depart in peace, according to your word; for my eyes have seen your salvation which you have prepared in the presence of all peoples, a light of revelation to the gentiles, and for the glory of your people Israel" (Lk. 2:29-32). Then, speaking to his Mother, Mary, he added: "Behold, this child is set for the fall and rising of many in Israel, and for a sign that is spoken against (and a sword shall pierce your own soul also), so that the thoughts of many hearts may be revealed" (Lk. 2:34-35).

Letter to Children, 1994

Together with Mary, let us seek to be *sharers* in this death which brought forth fruits of "new life" in the Resurrection: a death like this on the cross was infamous, and it was the death of her own Son! But precisely there, at the foot of the cross, "where she stood, not without a divine plan," did not Mary realize in a new way everything that she had already heard on the day of Annunciation?

Marian Year Letter to All Consecrated Persons, 1988

Consecrating ourselves to Mary means accepting her help to offer ourselves and the whole of mankind to him who is holy, infinitely holy; it means accepting her help — by having recourse to her motherly heart, which beneath the cross was opened to love for every human being, for the whole world — in order to offer the world, the individual human being, mankind as a whole, all the nations, to him who is infinitely holy. God's holiness showed itself in the redemption of man, of the world, of the whole of mankind, and of the nations; a redemption brought about through the sacrifice on the cross. "For their sake I consecrate myself," Jesus had said (Jn 17:19).

Address, Fátima, May 13, 1982

"When a woman is in travail she has sorrow, because her hour has come; but when she is delivered of the child, *she no longer remembers the anguish*, for joy that a child is born into the world" (Jn. 16:21). The first part of Christ's words refer to the "pangs of childbirth" which belong to the heritage of original sin; at the same time these words indicate *the link that exists between the woman's motherhood and the Paschal Mystery.* For this mystery also includes the Mother's sorrow at the foot of the cross — the Mother who through faith shares in her Son's amazing "self-emptying": "This is perhaps the deepest 'kenosis' of faith in human history."

As we contemplate this Mother, whose heart a sword has pierced (cf. Lk. 2:35), our thoughts go to *all suffering women in the world*, suffering either physically or morally. In this suffering a woman's sensitivity plays a role, even though she often succeeds in resisting suffering better than a man. It is difficult to enumerate these sufferings; it is difficult to call them by name. We may recall her maternal care for her children, especially when they fall sick or fall into bad ways; the death of those most dear to her; the loneliness of mothers forgotten by their grown-up children; the loneliness of widows; the sufferings of women who struggle alone to make a living; and women who have been wronged or exploited. Then there are the sufferings of consciences as a result of sin, which has wounded the woman's human or maternal dignity: the wounds of consciences which do not heal easily. With these sufferings, too, we must place ourselves at the foot of the cross.

Mulieris Dignitatem, 19

"Standing by the cross of Jesus was his mother" (Jn. 19:25). The Virgin, with her mother's grief, participated in a quite particular way in the Passion of Jesus, cooperating deeply with the salvation of mankind. Like Mary, each of us can and must unite with the suffering Jesus in order to become, with his own pain, an active part in the redemption of the world which he effected in the Paschal Mystery.

With these wishes, may my comforting blessing, strengthened by Mary's motherly help, accompany you and those who lovingly assist you in daily offering.

Audience, Rome, April 30, 1980

You have not suffered or do not suffer in vain. Pain matures you in spirit, purifies you in heart, gives you a real sense of the world and of life, enriches you with goodness, patience, and — hearing the Lord's promise reecho in your heart: "Blessed are those who mourn, for they shall be comforted" (Mt. 5:4) — gives you the sense of deep peace, perfect joy, and happy hope. Succeed, therefore, in giving a Christian value to your suffering, succeed in sanctifying your suffering with constant and generous hope in him who comforts and gives strength. I want you to know that you are not alone, or separated, or abandoned in your Via Crucis; beside you, each one of you, is the Blessed Virgin, who considers you her most beloved children: Mary, who "is a mother to us in the order of grace . . . from the consent which she loyally gave at the Annunciation and which she sustained without wavering beneath the cross. . ." (*Lumen Gentium*, 61-62), is close to you, because she greatly suffered with Jesus for the salvation of the world.

Look to her with full confidence and filial abandonment: she looks at you with a special glance; she smiles at you with motherly tenderness; she follows you with solicitous care!

Address, Lourdes, May 22, 1979

Turn your eyes incessantly to the Blessed Virgin; she, who is the Mother of Sorrows and also the Mother of Consolation, can understand you completely and help you.

Looking to her, praying to her, you will obtain that your tedium will become serenity, your anguish change into hope, and your grief into love. I accompany you with my blessing, which I willingly extend to all those who assist you.

Audience, Rome, October 31, 1979

Today's liturgy makes use of the ancient poetic text of the sequence which begins with the Latin words *Stabat Mater*:

> "By the cross of our salvation
> Mary stood in desolation
> While the Savior hung above
> All her human powers failing
> Sorrow's sword, at last prevailing,
> Stabs and breaks her heart of love. . .
> Virgin Mary, full of sorrow,
> From your love I ask to borrow
> Love enough to share your pain.
> Make my heart to burn with fire,
> Make Christ's love my one desire,
> Who for love of me was slain."

The author of this sequence sought, in the most eloquent way humanly possible, to present the "compassion" of the Mother at the foot of the cross. He was inspired by those words of Sacred Scripture about the sufferings of Mary which though few and concise, are deeply moving

Homily, Los Angeles, September 15, 1987

"Together with Mary, Mother of Christ who *stood beneath the cross,* we pause beside all the crosses of contemporary man and we ask all of you *who suffer* to support us. We ask precisely you who are weak to *become a source of strength* for the Church and humanity. In the terrible battle between the forces of good and evil revealed to our eyes by our modern world, may your sufferings in union with the cross of Christ be victorious."

Christifideles Laici, December 30, 1988

This woman of faith, Mary of Nazareth, the Mother of God, has been given to us as a model in our pilgrimage of faith. From Mary we learn to surrender to God's will in all things. From Mary we learn to trust even when all hope seems gone. From Mary we learn to love Christ, her Son and the Son of God. For Mary is not only the Mother of God, she is Mother of the Church as well. In every stage of the march through history, the Church has benefited from the prayer and protection of the Virgin Mary. Holy Scripture and the experience of the faithful see the Mother of God as the one who in a very special way is united with the Church at the most difficult moments in her history when Christ, and therefore his Church, provokes premeditated contradiction, Mary appears particularly close to the Church, because for her the Church is always her beloved Christ.

Address, Washington, D.C., October 6, 1979

The *Exultet* of Easter tells us that he is "the light which knows no decline," *"qui nescit occasum"!* Seek the light of the soul. Through it, suffering united with that of our Lord and of the Virgin Mary at the foot of the cross opens the way to eternal life, for oneself and for others.

Address, Lourdes, May 22, 1979

12 / Pillar of Faith

Through the faith of Mary, then, let us fix our gaze on *the mystery of Christ*. The mystery of the Son of Man, written in the earthly history of humanity, is at the same time the definitive manifestation of God in that history.

Simeon says: "This child is destined to be the downfall and the rise of many in Israel, a sign that will be opposed" (Lk. 2:34). How profound these words are! Into the history of us all: Christ is destined for the ruin and resurrection of many! Christ is a sign of contradiction! Is this not also true in our own time? In our age? *In our generation?*

And standing next to Christ is Mary. To her Simeon says: ". . . so that the thoughts of many hearts may be laid bare. And you yourself shall be pierced with a sword" (cf. Lk. 2:35).

Today we ask for *humility of heart* and for a clear conscience:

before God

through Christ.

Yes, we ask that the thoughts of our hearts may be laid bare. We ask that our *consciences may be pure*:

before God

through the cross of Christ
in the heart of Mary. Amen.
Homily, Los Angeles, September 15, 1987

The "yes" which she uttered at the Annunciation
was nothing but a confirmation of her previous
attitude, and the point of departure for a
journey in the Lord's company that lasted all
her life. In this way, Mary reminds religious of
the need to respond ever more generously to
the Lord's plans for them. Each one will give
this response in the first place by her openness
to the Holy Spirit, by her continual conversion
to Christ, by her chastity, poverty, and
obedience; in short by the unending discovery
of her vocation and mission in the Church.
Address, Manila, February 17, 1981

For every Christian, for every human being,
Mary is the one who first "believed," and
precisely with her faith as Spouse and Mother
she wishes to act upon all those who entrust
themselves to her as her children. And it is
well known that the more her children
persevere and progress in this attitude, the
nearer Mary leads them to the "unsearchable
riches of Christ" (Eph. 3:8).
Redemptoris Mater, 46

Mary says to us today: "I am the servant of the Lord. Let it be done to me as you say" (Lk. 1:38).

And with those words, she expresses what was *the fundamental attitude of her life: her faith!* Mary believed! She trusted in God's promises and was faithful to his will.

When the Archangel Gabriel announced that she was chosen to be the Mother of the Most High, she gave her *"fiat"* humbly and with full freedom, "Let it be done to me as you say."

Insegnamenti, October 6, 1979

The Council emphasizes that *the Mother of God is already the eschatological fulfillment of the Church:* "In the most holy Virgin the Church has already reached that perfection whereby she exists without spot or wrinkle (cf. Eph. 5:27)"; and at the same time the Council says that "the followers of Christ still strive to increase in holiness by conquering sin, and so *they raise their eyes to Mary, who* shines to the whole community of the elect as a model of the virtues." The pilgrimage of faith no longer belongs to the Mother of the Son of God: glorified at the side of her Son in heaven, Mary has already crossed the threshold between faith and the vision which is "face to face" (1

Cor. 13:12). At the same time, however, in this eschatological fulfillment, Mary does not cease to be the "Star of the Sea" (*Maris Stella*) for all those who are still on the journey of faith. If they lift their eyes to her from their earthly existence, they do so because "the Son whom she brought forth is he whom God placed as the firstborn among many brethren (Rom. 8:29)," and also because "in the birth and development" of these brothers and sisters, "she cooperates with a maternal love."

Redemptoris Mater, 6

The love of the Savior's Mother reaches every place touched by the work of salvation. Her care extends to every individual of our time, and to all the societies, nations, and peoples. Societies menaced by apostasy, threatened by moral degradation. The collapse of morality involves the collapse of societies.

Address, Fátima, May 13, 1982

But above all, in the Church of that time and of every time, Mary was and is the one who is "blessed because she believed"; *she was the first to believe.* From the moment of his birth in the stable at Bethlehem, Mary followed Jesus step by step in her maternal pilgrimage of faith. She followed him during the years of his hidden life at Nazareth; she followed him also during the time after he left home, when he began "to do and to teach" (cf. Acts 1:1) in the midst of Israel. Above all, she followed him in the tragic experience of Golgotha.

Redemptoris Mater, 26

We still carry in our hearts the serene joy of the mystery of Christ's birth which the Church's liturgy in this period has led us to celebrate and put into effect in our lives. Jesus of Nazareth, the Child cradled in the manger of Bethlehem, is the eternal Word of God who became incarnate for love of man (cf. Jn. 1:14). This is the great truth to which the Christian adheres with profound faith. With the faith of Mary most holy, who, in the glory of her intact virginity, conceived and brought forth the Son of God made man. With the faith of St. Joseph, who guarded and protected him with immense dedication of love. With the faith of the shepherds, who hastened immediately to the cave of the nativity. With the faith of the magi who glimpsed him in the sign of the star, and who, after a long search, were able to contemplate and adore him in the arms of the Virgin Mary.

Audience, Rome, January 7, 1981

As we celebrate Our Lady of Sorrows during the Marian Year, let us call to mind the teaching of the Second Vatican Council concerning the presence of Mary, the Mother God, in the mystery of Christ and the Church. Let us recall in particular the following words: "The Blessed Virgin advanced in her *pilgrimage of faith,* and loyally persevered in her union with her Son unto the cross, where she stood, in keeping with the divine plan" (*Lumen Gentium,* 56).

Mary's pilgrimage of faith! It is precisely at the foot of the cross that this pilgrimage of faith, which began at the Annunciation, *reaches its high point,* its culmination. There it is united with the agony of Mary's maternal heart. "Suffering grievously with her only-begotten Son . . . she lovingly consented to the immolation of this Victim which she herself had brought forth" (*Lumen Gentium,* 58). At the same time the agony of her maternal heart also represents a fulfillment of the words of Simeon: "And you yourself shall be pierced with a sword" (Lk. 2:35). Surely these prophetic words express the *"divine plan"* by which Mary is destined to stand at the foot of the cross.

Homily, Los Angeles, September 15, 1987

As the Council teaches, "The obedience of faith
(Rom. 16:26; cf. 1:5; 2 Cor. 10:5-6) must be
given to God who reveals, an obedience by
which man entrusts his whole self freely to
God." This description of faith found perfect
realization in Mary. The "decisive" moment was
the Annunciation, and the very words of
Elizabeth "And blessed is she who believed"
refer primarily to that very moment.

Indeed, at the Annunciation Mary
entrusted herself to God completely, with the
"full submission of intellect and will,"
manifesting "the obedience of faith" to him who
spoke to her through his messenger. She
responded, therefore, *with all her human and
feminine "I,"* and this response of faith
included both perfect cooperation with "the
grace of God that precedes and assists" and
perfect openness to the action of the Holy
Spirit, who "constantly brings faith to
completion by his gifts."

Redemptoris Mater, 13

The fundamental attitude in the life of the
Mother of God was one of faith. Mary trusted in
God's Providence. As Elizabeth said of her:
"Blessed is she who believed that there would
be a fulfillment of what was spoken to her from

the Lord" (Lk. 1:45). I pray that your lives will likewise be marked by a deep faith in the Providence of God. Then, with trusting surrender to the Lord's will in all things, you will be hope-filled witnesses of Christ in the world. May Mary obtain this grace for you. And may her Divine Son bless you with his peace.

Address to Marists, Rome, September 27, 1985

To Mary, who is the Mother of divine grace, I entrust priestly and religious vocations. May the new spring of vocations, their new increase throughout the Church, become a particular proof of her motherly presence in the mystery of Christ, in our times, and in the mystery of his Church all over the earth. *Mary alone is a living incarnation of that total and complete dedication to God, to Christ in his salvific action, which must find its adequate expression in every priestly and religious vocation. Mary is the fullest expression of perfect faithfulness to the Holy Spirit and to his action in the soul; she is the expression of the faithfulness which means persevering cooperation in the grace of vocation.*

Audience, Rome, May 2, 1979

May you who have received so much from God *hear the call to a renewal of your Christian life and to fidelity to the faith of your fathers.* May you respond in the spirit of Mary, the Virgin Mother whom the Church sees "maternally present and sharing in the many complicated problems which today beset the lives of individuals, families, and nations . . . helping the Christian people in the constant struggle between good and evil, to ensure that it 'does not fall,' or if it has fallen that it 'rises again' " (*Redemptoris Mater*, 52).

Homily, San Antonio, September 13, 1987

This ineffable meeting with the personal and living God can take place only in the darkness of faith. The Groom stands behind the door while you are still outside in the night. It is always in the light of faith that God gives himself. But the signs of God are so discreet in the ordinariness of your everyday life that you must be vigilant if you are to persevere and grow in faith in imitation of Mary. The "treasure" that awaits you in heaven will only be the eschatological fulfillment of what is hidden in the inner "treasure" of the heart (cf. *Redemptionis Donum*, 5).

Homily, Quebec, September 19, 1984

Now, at the first dawn of the Church, at the beginning of the long journey through faith which began at Pentecost in Jerusalem, Mary was with all those who were the seed of the "new Israel." She was present among them as an exceptional witness to the mystery of Christ. And the Church was assiduous in prayer together with her, and at the same time *"contemplated her in the light of the Word made man."* It was always to be so. For when the Church "enters more intimately into the supreme mystery of the Incarnation," she thinks of the Mother of Christ with profound reverence and devotion. Mary belongs indissolubly to the mystery of Christ, and she belongs also to the mystery of the Church from the beginning, from the day of the Church's birth. At the basis of what the Church has been from the beginning, and of what she must continually become from generation to generation, in the midst of all the nations of the earth, we find the one "who believed that there would be a fulfillment of what was spoken to her from the Lord" (Lk. 1:45). It is precisely Mary's faith which marks the beginning of the new and eternal Covenant of God with man in Jesus Christ; this heroic *faith* of hers *"precedes"* the apostolic *witness* of the Church, and ever remains in the Church's heart, hidden like a special heritage of God's

revelation. All those who from generation to generation accept the apostolic witness of the Church share in that mysterious inheritance, and *in a sense share in Mary's faith.*
Redemptoris Mater, 27

"Blessed is she who believed that there would be a fulfillment of what was spoken to her from the Lord" (Lk. 1:45). So said Elizabeth, answering our Lady's greeting. They are words dictated by the Holy Spirit (cf. Lk. 1:41). They highlight Mary's main virtue: faith. The Fathers of the Church stopped to reflect on the meaning of this virtue in the spiritual life of the Virgin and they did not hesitate to express evaluations which may seem surprising to us. Let it suffice to quote St. Augustine for them all: "Her relationship as mother would not have benefited Mary in any way, if she had not borne Christ more richly in her heart than in her body" (*De Sancta Virgine*, 3:3).

Faith permitted Mary to approach fearlessly the unexplored abyss of God's plan of salvation: it was not easy to believe that God could "become flesh" and come to "dwell among us" (cf. Jn. 1:14), that is, that *he wished to conceal himself in the insignificance of our daily life, donning our human frailty, subject to so many and such humiliating conditions.* Mary dared to believe in this "impossible" plan; she trusted the Almighty and became the main collaborator of that admirable divine initiative which reopened our history to hope.

Address, Rome, February 11, 1981

The Holy Spirit, who with his power overshadowed the virginal body of *Mary*, bringing about in her *the beginning of her divine motherhood*, at the same time made her heart perfectly obedient to that self-communication of God which surpassed every human idea and faculty. "Blessed is she who believed!": thus Mary is greeted by her cousin Elizabeth, herself "full of the Holy Spirit." In the words of greeting addressed to *her "who believed"* we seem to detect a distant (but in fact very close) contrast with all those about whom Christ will say that "they do not believe." Mary entered the history of the salvation of the world through the obedience of faith. And *faith*, in its deepest essence, is *the openness* of the human heart to the gift: *to God's self-communication in the Holy Spirit.* St. Paul writes: "The Lord is the Spirit, and where the Spirit of the Lord is, there is freedom." When the Triune God opens himself to man in the Holy Spirit, this opening of God reveals and also gives to the human creature the fullness of freedom. This fullness was manifested in a sublime way precisely through the faith of Mary, through the "obedience of faith": truly, "Blessed is she who believed!"

Dominum et Vivificantem, 49

The Blessed Virgin who will be, as it were, "indirectly" present in the whole preparatory phase, will be contemplated in . . . the mystery of her divine motherhood. It was in her womb that the Word became flesh! The affirmation of the central place of Christ cannot therefore be separated from the recognition of the role played by his most holy Mother. Veneration of her, when properly understood, can in no way take away from her "the dignity and efficacy of Christ the one mediator." Mary in fact constantly points to her Divine Son and she is proposed to all believers as the *model of faith* which is put into practice. Devotedly meditating on her and contemplating her in the light of the Word made man, the Church with reverence enters more intimately into the supreme mystery of the Incarnation and becomes ever increasingly like her Spouse.

Tertio Millennio Adveniente, 43

The Mother of *that Son,* therefore, mindful of what has been told her at the Annunciation and in subsequent events, bears within herself the radical "newness" of faith: *the beginning of the New Covenant.* This is the beginning of the Gospel, the joyful Good News. However, it is not difficult to see in that beginning *a particular heaviness of heart,* linked with a sort of "night of faith" — to use the words of St. John of the Cross — a kind of "veil" through which one has to draw near to the Invincible One and to live in intimacy with the mystery. And this is the way that Mary, for many years, *lived in intimacy with the mystery of her Son,* and went forward in her "pilgrimage of faith," while Jesus "increased in wisdom . . . and in favor with God and man" (Lk. 2:52). God's predilection for him was manifested ever more clearly to people's eyes. The first human creature thus permitted to discover Christ was Mary, who lived with Joseph in the same house at Nazareth.

Redemptoris Mater, 17

May your thoughts and resolutions, dear brothers and sisters, be centered today on the great fidelity to which you are called: fidelity to union, fidelity to the Eucharist, fidelity to hope. This fidelity is essential to our baptismal calling, to our vocation, to our consecration. This fidelity embraces a whole attitude, a whole program of life; it is, moreover, an indispensable basis for any apostolate at the service of the Gospel. And may Mary, *Virgo fidelis*, sustain you in this fidelity, keeping you faithful to Jesus forever.

Homily, Taiwan, November 11, 1980

When Luke the Evangelist describes the Lord's Ascension to the disciples who were "persevering with one mind" in prayer, he specifically says: "with Mary the Mother of Jesus" (Acts 1:14). She, the Mother of the Lord, the Mother of all the faithful, the Mother, too, of priests, wants to be with us so that we can ever again be sent in the Holy Spirit into this world and to the people with their troubles.

Homily, Fulda, Germany, November 17, 1980

Among the many titles bestowed on the Virgin throughout the centuries by the filial love of Christians, there is one that has a very deep meaning: *Virgo fidelis*, the faithful Virgin. What does this faithfulness of Mary's mean? What are the dimensions of this faithfulness?

The first dimension is called *search*. Mary was faithful first of all when she began, lovingly, to seek the deep sense of God's plan in her and for the world. *"Quomodo fiet?"* — "How shall this be?" — she asked the angel of the Annunciation. Already in the Old Testament the meaning of this search is portrayed in an expression of outstanding beauty and extraordinary spiritual content: "To seek the face of the Lord." There will not be faithfulness if it is not rooted in this ardent, patient, and generous search; if there is not in man's heart a question to which only God gives an answer, or rather, to which only God is the answer.

The second dimension of faithfulness is called *reception,* acceptance. The *"quomodo fiet?"* is changed, on Mary's lips, to *"fiat."* Let it be done, I am ready, I accept: this is the crucial moment of faithfulness, the moment in which man perceives that he will never completely understand the "how"; that there are in God's plan more areas of mystery than of clarity; that, however he may try, he will never succeed in understanding it completely. It is then that man accepts the mystery, gives it a place in his heart, just as "Mary kept all these things, pondering them in her heart" (Lk. 2:19; cf. Lk. 3:15). It is the moment when man abandons himself to the mystery, not with the resignation of one who capitulates before an enigma or an absurdity, but rather with the availability of one who opens up to be inhabited by something — by Someone! — greater than his own heart. This acceptance takes place, in short, through faith, which is the adherence of the whole being to the mystery that is revealed.

The third dimension of faithfulness is *consistency*: to live in accordance with what one believes, to adapt one's life to the object of one's adherence. To accept persecutions or misunderstandings rather than a break between what one practices and what one believes: this is consistency. Here is, perhaps, the deepest core of faithfulness.

But all faithfulness must pass the more exacting test: that of duration. Therefore the fourth dimension of faithfulness is *constancy*. It is easy to be consistent for a day or two. It is difficult and important to be consistent for one's whole life. It is easy to be consistent on the hour of enthusiasm; it is difficult to be so in the hour of tribulation. And only a consistency that lasts throughout the whole of life can be called faithfulness. Mary's *"fiat"* in the Annunciation finds its fullness in the silent *"fiat"* that she repeats at the foot of the cross. To be faithful means not betraying in the darkness what one has accepted in public.

Address, Mexico City, January 26, 1979

13 / Queen of All Saints

In order to live for Christ and no longer for ourselves, to collaborate in the ministry of reconciliation, to build the kingdom of God, we must bear the cross and follow Christ. Let us not be afraid to be signs of contradiction. Let us embrace the cross, confident that it is a "tree of eternal life," trusting in the firm promise of resurrection.

Together with the Virgin Mary and all the saints, let us build God's kingdom here on earth, so as to be able to live for ever with the Father, and the Son, and the Holy Spirit. Amen.

Homily, Port Moresby, New Guinea, May 8, 1984

As the Council teaches, the Mother of God is the Christian's model in faith, love, and perfect union with Christ (cf. *Lumen Gentium*, 63); and in a special way she is the Mother and the model of those who live the consecrated life.

Address, Manila, February 17, 1981

. . . I wish in particular to bring the youth of the whole world and of the whole Church closer to her, to Mary who is the Mother of fair love. She bears within her an indestructible sign of youth and beauty which never pass. I wish and pray that the young will approach her, have confidence in her, and entrust to her the life that is before them; that they will love her with a simple and warm love of the heart. She alone is capable of responding to this love in the best way:

> "Following Mary you will not go astray, calling upon Mary you will not despair, thinking of Mary, you will not err. . . , turning to Mary, you will have her favor. . . ."
>
> (St. Bernard, *Homilia II super Missus est,* XVII: PL 183, 71)
>
> **Audience, Rome, May 2, 1979**

I entrust these wishes and this prayer to the powerful intercession of Mary, Queen of Apostles, in the hope that those who are called will be able to discern and follow generously the voice of the Divine Master, and I invoke upon you, dear brothers in the episcopate, and upon you, dear sons and daughters of the whole Church, the gifts of the Redeemer's peace and serenity. And with all my heart I impart to you the apostolic blessing.

Audience, Rome, May 5, 1979

Mary is the radiant sign and inviting model of the moral life. As St. Ambrose put it, "The life of this one person can serve as a model for everyone," and while speaking specifically to virgins but within a context open to all he affirmed: "The first stimulus to learning is the nobility of the teacher. Who can be more noble than the Mother of God? Who can be more glorious than the one chosen by glory itself? Mary lived and exercised her freedom precisely by giving herself to God and accepting God's gift within herself. Until the time of his birth she sheltered in her womb the Son of God who became man, she raised him and enabled him to grow, and she accompanied him in that supreme act of freedom which is the complete sacrifice of his own life. By the gift of herself, Mary entered fully into the plan of God, who gives himself to the world. By accepting and pondering in her heart events which she did not always understand (cf. Lk. 2:19) she became the model of all those who hear the Word of God and keep it (cf. Lk. 11:28), and merited the title of "Seat of Wisdom."

Veritatis Splendor, 120

Finally, I entrust you to the intercession of the holy martyrs of Nagasaki, and especially to the protection of Mary, Queen of Martyrs and Mother of the Church. She is indeed the Mother of all Christians, especially of those who lead the religious life, she who is so venerated in Japan as Edo no Santa Maria and as Our Lady of Otometoge.

Address, Nagasaki, February 26, 1981

In one of her apparitions to St. Catherine Labouré, our Lady said to the young sister — frightened by the greatness and the difficulty of the mission which had been entrusted to her — "It is here at the foot of the tabernacle that you must seek the strength and consolation!" The heavenly Mother addresses the same words to each of you. With the Eucharist, near the tabernacle, may you be holy and fearless sisters, today and for the rest of your lives!

Address, Milan, May 20, 1983

I conclude by entrusting you to the Virgin Mary, to whom St. Bernardine was extremely devoted and whom, it can be said, he went proclaiming all over Italy every day. Having lost his own mother, he chose our Lady as his mother and always lavished his affection on her and trusted completely in her. He became the singer of Mary's beauty, it can be affirmed, and preaching her meditation with inspired love, he was not afraid to state: "Every grace that is given to men proceeds from a triple ordained cause: from God it passes to Christ, from Christ it passes to the Virgin, from the Virgin it is given to us" (*Sermo VI in festis B.V.M. De Annun.* a. 1, c. 2).

Turn to her every day with confidence and with love, and ask her for the grace of the beauty of your soul and of your life, of what alone can make you happy.

With these wishes, invoking the intercession of St. Bernardine, I impart to you the apostolic blessing. May it always accompany you as a sign of my deepest affection.

Address, Abruzzi, Italy, August 30, 1980

Still feeling the intense joy caused last Sunday by the solemn ceremony of three beatifications, while I extend to you, beloved young people, my special greeting, I repeat to you some words that Don Luigi Orione wrote to his young followers: "I pray humbly but with filial confidence to the Blessed Virgin Mary so that she may assist you and comfort you, so that

---

she may save you from discouragement. . ."
(Letter of August 21, 1939). And on another
occasion he exclaimed: "O young people! Hail
Mary, always! . . . Hail Mary, and forward! . . .
Hail Mary, until blessed Paradise!" (Writing of
May, 1923).

I, too, willingly leave you this exhortation
and this program of life together with my
blessing.

Address, Rome, October 29, 1980

In the name of Jesus let us go forth
confidently, and in the name of Mary let us
rejoice. St. Paul Miki and his companion
martyrs understood the meaning of these
names and their gentle power. And may this
heritage long remain in Japan: to lead future
generations to Jesus through Mary.

Dear brothers, thank you for your
invitation to come to Japan. Thank you for
your own fraternal support and for your
partnership in the Gospel. "My love be with
you all in Christ Jesus. Amen" (cf. 1 Cor.
16:24).

Address, Tokyo, February 23, 1981

As we ourselves pursue every day the justice
and holiness born of truth, let us look to Mary,

Mother of Jesus, Queen of the Apostles, and cause of our joy. May St. Frances Xavier Cabrini, St. Elizabeth Ann Seton, and St. John Neumann pray for you, and for all the people who you are called to serve in holiness and truth and in the unity of Christ and his Church.

Homily, Chicago, October 5, 1979

For how many children in the history of the Church has the Eucharist been a source of spiritual strength, sometimes even heroic strength! How can we fail *to be reminded,* for example, *of holy boys and girls* who lived in the first centuries and are still known and venerated throughout the Church? St. Agnes, who lived in Rome; St. Agatha, who was martyred in Sicily; St. Tarcisius, a boy who is rightly called the "martyr of the Eucharist" because he preferred to die rather than give up Jesus, whom he was carrying under the appearance of bread.

And so down the centuries, up to our own times, *there are many boys and girls among those declared by the Church to be saints or blessed.* Just as Jesus in the Gospel shows special trust in children, so his Mother, Mary, in the course of history, has not failed to show *her motherly care for the little ones.* Think of St.

Bernadette of Lourdes, the children of La Salette, and, in our own century, Lucia, Francisco, and Jacinta of Fátima.

Letter to Children, 1994

The woman becomes also, by association with her Son, the sign of contradiction to the world, and at the same time the sign of hope, whom all generations shall call blessed. The woman who conceived spiritually before she conceived physically, the woman who accepted the Word of God, the woman who was inserted intimately and irrevocably into the mystery of the Church, exercising a spiritual motherhood with regard to all peoples. The woman who is honored as Queen of the Apostles, without herself being inserted into the hierarchical constitution of the Church, and yet this woman made all hierarchy possible because she gave to the world the Shepherd and Bishop of our souls. This woman, this Mary of the Gospels, who is not mentioned as being at the Last Supper, comes back again at the foot of the cross, in order to consummate her contribution to salvation history. By her courageous act she prefigures and anticipates the courage of all women throughout the ages who concur in bringing forth Christ in every generation.

At Pentecost, the Virgin Mary once again

comes forward to exercise her role in union with the Apostles, with and in and over the Church. Yet again, she conceived of the Holy Spirit to bring forth Jesus in the fullness of his Body, the Church, never to leave him, never to abandon him, but to continue to love and to cherish him through the ages.

Address, Washington, D.C., October 7, 1979

Our communion is a communion of prayer, in which we all draw strength from the whole praying Body of Christ. The activity of prayer is very much a part of the life of the Church, uniting us with the living and the dead in the communion of saints. The saints of God are our intercessors. In particular, the Mother of Jesus, who is the Mother of the whole Body, intercedes for all who have received life in her Son. Legions of Christian faithful fulfill an ecclesial role of inestimable value by praying for the Church and her mission. We count on all these prayers, and are especially grateful for the contribution of the sick and the suffering.

Address, Rome, May 26, 1980

This *ad limina* visit, venerable brothers, is also a celebration of faith: the faith of the whole Church in Japan — the faith of which you, in nion with the successor of Peter, are guardians and authentic teachers. On my part oday I wish to render homage to this faith, hich through missionary efforts was implanted by God as his gift in the hearts of the faithful. This gift of faith was generously accepted and genuinely lived. It became the object of the witnessing of Paul Miki and his martyr companions, who went to their death proclaiming the names of Jesus and Mary, and who by their martyrdom confirmed the Faith as the everlasting heritage in Japan. By the grace of God and the help of his Blessed Mother, this Catholic Faith was, moreover, preserved throughout generations by the Japanese laity who maintained by the instinct of faith their unbreakable attachment to the See of Peter.

Address to Japanese Bishops, Rome, May 20, 1980

. . . Mary is present in the Church to stimulate the holiness of her best sons, to direct them along heroic ways of evangelical and missionary surrender in favor of the poor, children, the simple, the suffering, those who are waiting for Christ's message. Mary is the inspirer of holiness in the Church, and we find a moving confirmation of this also in those new Blesseds, whom the Lord has given me the incomparable consolation of holding up to the devotion and admiration of the faithful of the whole world: Francis Coll, James Laval, Henry de Osso y Cervello, Joseph de Anchieta, Mary of the Incarnation (Guyart), Peter de Betancur, Francis de Montmorency-Laval, Kateri Tekakwitha.

Address, Rome, Feast of Sts. Peter and Paul, 1980

14 / Queen of Peace

So, Mother most holy, with the peace of God in our consciences, with our hearts free of malice and hate, we shall be able to bring true joy and true peace to all, which come from your Son, our Lord Jesus Christ, who lives and reigns with the Father and the Holy Spirit forever and ever. Amen.

Address, Mexico City, January 12, 1979

May the Virgin Mary, who is the Mother of the Church, also be the Mother of "the Church of the home." Thanks to her motherly aid, may each Christian family become a "little Church" in which the mystery of the Church of Christ is mirrored and given new life. May she, the handmaid of the Lord, be an example of humble and generous acceptance of the will of God. May she, the Sorrowful Mother at the foot of the cross, comfort the sufferings and dry the tears of those in distress because of the difficulties of their families.

Familiaris Consortio, 86

In order that this unity and the constant and systematic collaboration which leads to it may be perseveringly continued, I beg on my knees that, through the intercession of Mary, holy spouse of the Holy Spirit and Mother of the Church, we may all receive the light of the Holy Spirit. And blessing everyone, with all my heart I once more address myself to you . . . with a fraternal greeting and with full trust. . . . Let us do all we can to ensure that the Eucharist may become an ever greater source of life and light for the consciences of all our brothers and sisters of all the communities in the universal unity of Christ's Church on earth.

Dominicae Cenae, 13

I entrust to Our Lady, Queen of Peace, the title by which you invoke her in this land. She is the Mother of all, the example of a commitment to God's will and to the history of her people. I ask her to help you in your ministry of reconciliation, in your mission of evangelization, to be, with your commitment, authentic disciples of Christ. Amen.

Homily, San Salvador, March 6, 1983

Brothers and sisters, there is one who walks beside us along the path of discipleship: Mary, the Mother of Jesus, who pondered everything in her heart and always did the will of the Father (cf. Lk. 2:51; Mk. 3:35). In this metropolitan cathedral dedicated to her, I wish to return to the thoughts and sentiments that filled my heart at Fátima on May 13. There I once again consecrated to her myself and my ministry: *Totus tuus ego sum.* I reconsecrated and entrusted to her maternal protection the Church and the whole world, so much in need of wisdom and peace.

These are some of the invocations I addressed to the Immaculate Heart of Mary at Fátima:

From famine and war, *deliver us.*

From nuclear war, from incalculable self-destruction, from every kind of war, *deliver us.*

From sins against the life of man from its very beginning, *deliver us.*

From hatred and from the demeaning of the dignity of the children of God, *deliver us.*

From every kind of injustice in the life of society, both national and international, *deliver us.*

From readiness to trample on the commandments of God, *deliver us.*

From attempts to stifle in human hearts the very truth of God, *deliver us.*

From sins against the Holy Spirit, *deliver us.*

Accept, O Mother of Christ, this cry laden with the suffering of all individual human beings, laden with the suffering of whole societies.

Let there be revealed, once more, in the history of the world the infinite power of merciful love. May it put a stop to evil. May it transform consciences. May your Immaculate Heart reveal for all the light of hope.

Address, Edinburgh Cathedral, May 31, 1982

Mary, Queen of Peace, is close to the women of our day because of her motherhood, her example of openness to others' needs, and her witness of suffering. Mary lived with a deep sense of responsibility the plan which God willed to carry out in her for the salvation of all humanity. When she was made aware of the miracle which God had worked in her by making her the Mother of his Incarnate Son, her first thought was to visit her elderly kinswoman Elizabeth in order to help her. That meeting gave Mary the chance to express, in the marvelous canticle of the *Magnificat* (Lk. 1:46-55), her gratitude to God who, with her and through her, had begun a new creation, a new history.

I implore the most holy Virgin Mary to

sustain those men and women who, in the service of life, have committed themselves to building peace. With her help, may they bear witness before all people, especially those who live in darkness and suffering and who hunger and thirst for justice, to the loving presence of the God of peace!

Address, Rome, December 8, 1994

15 / Seat of Wisdom

O Mary,
Mother of Jesus Christ and Mother of
    priests,
accept this title which we bestow on you
to celebrate your motherhood
and to contemplate with you the priesthood
of your Son and your sons,
O holy Mother of God.
O Mother of Christ,
to the Messiah-Priest you gave a body of
    flesh
through the anointing of the Holy Spirit
for the salvation of the poor and the
    contrite of heart;
guard priests in your heart and in the
    Church,
O Mother of the Savior.
O Mother of Faith,
you accompanied to the Temple the Son of
    Man,
the fulfillment of the promises given to the
    fathers;
give to the Father for his glory
the priests of your Son,
O Ark of the Covenant.
O Mother of the Church,

in the midst of the disciples in the Upper
    Room
you prayed to the Spirit
for the new people and their shepherds;
obtain for the Order of Presbyters
a full measure of gifts,
O Queen of the Apostles.
O Mother of Jesus Christ,
you were with him at the beginning
of his life and mission,
you sought the Master among the crowd,
you stood beside him when he was lifted
up from the earth
consumed as the one eternal Sacrifice,
and you had John, your son, near at hand;
accept from the beginning those
who have been called,
protect their growth,
in their life ministry accompany
your sons,
O Mother of Priests.
Amen.

Pastores Dabo Vobis, 82

Be faithful to the Mother of fair love. Have trust
in her, as you shape your love and form your
young families.

May Christ always be for you "the Way, the
Truth, and the Life."

Address, Kraków, June 8, 1979

The cross is the living book from which we learn definitively who we are and how we must act. This book is always open in front of us. Read, reflect, enjoy this new wisdom. Make it your own and you will walk also along the paths of knowledge, culture, and university life, spreading light in a service of love, worthy of children of God.

And look also to the Blessed Virgin, standing by the cross of Jesus (Jn. 19:25), where she is given to us as our mother: she is our hope, the seat of true Wisdom.

And may the Lord accompany you every day, sustain your witness, and make your work fruitful.

On my part, I willingly grant you the apostolic blessing, which propitiates abundant heavenly favors; and I invite you to extend it to your friends and to all your dear ones.

Address, Rome, April 1, 1980

Like the Apostles after Christ's Ascension, the Church must gather in the Upper Room "together with Mary, the Mother of Jesus" (Acts 1:14), in order to pray for the Spirit and to gain strength and courage to carry out the missionary mandate. We, too, like the Apostles, need to be transformed and guided by the Spirit.

On the eve of the third millennium the whole Church is invited to live more intensely the mystery of Christ by gratefully cooperating in the work of salvation. The Church does this together with Mary and following the example of Mary, the Church's Mother and model: Mary is the model of that maternal love which should inspire all who cooperate in the Church's apostolic mission for the rebirth of humanity. Therefore, "strengthened by the presence of Christ, the Church journeys through time toward the consummation of the ages and goes to meet the Lord who comes. But on this journey . . . she proceeds along *the path* already trodden by the Virgin Mary."

Redemptionis Missio, 92

When the Holy Family returns to Nazareth after Herod's death, there begins the long *period of the hidden life.* She "who believed that there would be a fulfillment of what was spoken to her from the Lord" (Lk. 1:45) lives the reality of these words day by day. And daily at her side is the Son to whom *"she gave the name Jesus";* therefore in contact with him she certainly uses his name, a fact which would have surprised no one, since the name had long been in use in Israel. Nevertheless, Mary knows that he who bears the name *Jesus has been called by the angel "the Son of the Most High"* (cf. Lk. 1:32). Mary knows she has conceived and given birth to him "without having a husband," by the power of the Holy Spirit, by the power of the Most High who overshadowed her (cf. Lk. 1:35), just as at the time of Moses and the patriarchs the cloud covered the presence of God (cf. Ex. 24:16, 40:34-35; 1 Kgs. 8:10-12). Therefore Mary knows that the Son to whom she gave birth in a virginal manner is precisely that "Holy One," the Son of God, of whom the angel spoke to her.

During the years of Jesus' hidden life in the house at Nazareth, *Mary's life too is "hidden with Christ in God"* (cf. Col 3:3) *through faith.* For faith is contact with the mystery of God Every day Mary is in constant contact with the ineffable mystery of God made man, a mystery that surpasses everything revealed in the Old Covenant. From the moment of the Annunciation, the mind of the Virgin-Mother has been initiated into the radical "newness" of God's self-revelation and has been made aware of the mystery. She is the first of those "little ones" of whom Jesus will say one day: "Father, . . . you have hidden these things from the wise and understanding and revealed them to babes" (Mt. 11:25). For "no one knows the Son except the Father" (Mt. 11:27). If this is the case, how can Mary "know the Son"? Of course she does not know him as the Father does; and yet she is *the first of those to whom the Father "has chosen to reveal him"* (cf. Mt. 11:26-27; 1 Cor. 2:11). If though, from the moment of the Annunciation, the Son — whom only the Father knows completely, as the one who begets him in the eternal "today" (cf. Ps. 2:7) — was revealed to Mary, she, his Mother, is in contact with the truth about her Son only in faith and through faith! She is therefore blessed, because "she has believed," and continues to *believe day after day* amidst all the trials and the adversities of Jesus' infancy and then during the years of the hidden life at Nazareth, where he "was obedient to them" (Lk. 2:51). He was obedient both to Mary and also to Joseph, since Joseph took the place of his Father in people's eyes; for this reason, the Son of Mary was regarded by the people as "the carpenter's son" (Mt. 13:55).

Redemptoris Mater, 17

The fullness of the Spirit of God is accompanied by many different gifts, the treasures of salvation, destined in a particular way for the poor and suffering, for all those who open their hearts to these gifts — sometimes through the painful experience of their own existence — but first of all through the interior availability which comes from faith. The aged Simeon, the "righteous and devout man" upon whom "rested the Holy Spirit," sensed this at the moment of Jesus' presentation in the Temple, when he perceived in him the "salvation . . . prepared in the presence of all peoples" at the price of the great suffering — the cross — which he would have to embrace together with his Mother. The Virgin Mary, who "had conceived by the Holy Spirit," sensed this even more clearly, when she pondered in her heart the "mysteries" of the Messiah, with whom she was associated.

Dominum et Vivificantem, 4

To succeed in your intention, entrust yourselves to the Blessed Virgin Mary always, but especially in moments of difficulty and darkness. "From Mary we learn to surrender to God's will in all things. From Mary we learn to trust even when all hope seems gone. From Mary we learn to love Christ, her Son and the Son of God. . . . Learn from her to be always faithful, to trust that God's Word to you will be fulfilled, and that nothing is impossible with God."

Address, Washington, D.C., October 6, 1979

Beloved young people! Continue to live in the truth and for the truth! May the Blessed Virgin, the Seat of Wisdom, Mother of the Word who enlightens every man, assist you, enlighten you, and comfort you.

Address, Rome, November 25, 1979

It is a joy that springs from amazement at the almighty power of God, who can permit himself to carry out "great things," in spite of the inadequacy of human instruments (cf. Lk. 1:47-49). It is a joy at the superior justice of God, who "has put down the mighty from their thrones, and exalted those of low degree; he has filled the hungry with good things, and the rich he has sent away" (Lk. 1:52f). It is, finally, joy at the mercy of God who, faithful to his promises, gathers under the wing of his love the children of Abraham, "from generation to generation," assisting them in all their necessities (cf. Lk. 1:50, 54-55).

This is Mary's song. It must become the song of every day of our life; there is no human situation, in fact, that cannot find in it adequate interpretation. The Virgin utters it while over her spirit there thicken questions about the reactions of her betrothed, who still knows nothing about the future of this Son, over whom there hang disquieting prophetic words (cf. Is. 53).

Homily, Rome, February 11, 1981

The prophecy and the promise of faith, whose fulfillment was awaited by the whole people, the Israel of divine election, and the whole of humanity: This was Mary's mystery. Joseph did not know this mystery. She could not transmit it to him, because it was a mystery beyond the capacity of the human intellect and the possibilities of human language. It was not possible to transmit it by any human means. It was only possible to accept it from God — and believe. Just as Mary believed.

Address, Termi, Italy, March 19, 1981

The Church, which was once born in the Pentecost Upper Room, continues to be born in every upper room of prayer. She is born to become our spiritual mother in the likeness of the Mother of the eternal Word. She is born to reveal the characteristics and power of that motherhood (the motherhood of the Mother of God) thanks to which we can "be called children of God; and so we are" (1 Jn. 3:1). For, in his plan of salvation, the holy fatherhood of

God used the virginal motherhood of his lowly handmaiden to bring about in the children of man the work of the Divine Author.

Dear fellow-countrymen, venerable and beloved brothers in the episcopate, pastors of the Church in Poland, illustrious guests, and all of you the faithful: consent that I, as St. Peter's successor present with you here today, should entrust the whole of the Church to the Mother of Christ with the same lively faith, the same heroic hope, with which we did so on the memorable day of May 3 of the Polish millennium.

Consent that I should bring here, as I did already in the Basilica of St. Mary Major in Rome and later in the shrine of Guadalupe in Mexico, the mysteries of the hearts, the sorrow and suffering, and finally the hope and expectation of this final period of the twentieth century of the Christian era.

Consent that I should *entrust* all this to Mary.

Consent that I should entrust it to her in a new and solemn way.

I am a man of great trust.

I learnt to be so here.

Amen.

Homily, Jasna Góra, June 4, 1979

16 / Star of the Sea

O Mary,
bright dawn of the new world,
Mother of the living,
to you do we entrust the *cause of life*:
Look down, O Mother,
upon the vast numbers
of babies not allowed to be born,
of the poor whose lives are made difficult,
of men and women
who are victims of brutal violence,
of the elderly and the sick killed
by indifference or out of misguided mercy.
Grant that all who believe in your Son
may *proclaim the Gospel of life*
with honesty and love
to the people of our time.
Obtain for them the grace
to *accept that Gospel*
as a gift ever new,
the joy *of celebrating* it with gratitude
throughout their lives
and the courage to *bear witness to it*
resolutely, in order to build,
together with all people of good will,
the civilization of truth and love,

to the praise and glory of God,
the Creator and lover of life.
   Evangelium Vitae, **105**

I entrust you all to Mary most holy, our Mother
in heaven, the Star of the Sea of our life: pray
to her every day, you children! Give your hand
to Mary most holy, so that she may lead you to
receive Jesus in a holy way.
   Address, Rome, June 14, 1979

The Virgin Mother is constantly present on this
journey of faith of the People of God toward the
light. This is shown in a special way by the
canticle of the *Magnificat*, which, *welled up
from the depths of Mary's faith* at the
Visitation, ceaselessly reechoes in the heart of
the Church down the centuries. This is proved
by its daily recitation in the liturgy of the
Vespers and at many other moments of both
personal and communal devotion.
   "My soul magnifies the Lord,
   and my spirit rejoices in God my Savior,
   for he has looked on his servant in her
      lowliness.
   For Behold, henceforth all generations will
      call me blessed;

for he who is mighty has done great things
  for me,
and holy is his name;
and his mercy is from age to age
on those who fear him.
He has shown strength with his arm,
he has scattered the proud-hearted,
he has cast down the mighty from their
  thrones,
and lifted up the lowly;
he has filled the hungry with good things,
sent the rich away empty.
He has helped his servant Israel,
remembering his mercy,
as he spoke to our fathers,
to Abraham and to his posterity for ever."
(Lk. 1:46-55)

Redemptoris Mater, 36

All her earthly life was a "pilgrimage of faith."
For, like us, she walked in shadows and hoped
for things unseen. She knew the contradictions
of our earthly life. She was promised that her
Son would be given David's throne; but, at his
birth, there was no room even at the inn. Mary
still believed. The angel said her child would be
called the Son of God; but she would see him
slandered, betrayed, condemned, and left to die
as a thief on the cross.

Even yet, Mary "trusted that the Lord's words to her would be fulfilled" (Lk. 1:45) and that "nothing is impossible with God" (Lk. 1:37).

This woman of faith, Mary of Nazareth, the Mother of God, has been given to us as *a model in our pilgrimage of faith.* From Mary, we learn to surrender to God's will in all things.

Insegnamenti, **October 6, 1979**

If the mystery of the Word made flesh enables us to glimpse the mystery of the divine motherhood, and if, in turn, contemplation of the Mother of God brings us a more profound understanding of the mystery of the Incarnation, then the same must be said for the mystery of the Church and Mary's role in the work of salvation. By a more profound study of both Mary and the Church, clarifying each by the light of the other, Christians who are eager to do what Jesus tells them — as their Mother recommends (cf. Jn. 2:5) — will be able to go forward together on this "pilgrimage of faith." Mary, who is still the model of this pilgrimage, is to lead them to the unity which is willed by their one Lord and so much desired by those who are attentively listening to what "the Spirit is saying to the Churches" today (Rev. 2:7, 11, 17).

Redemptoris Mater, **20**

We are all journeying along the roads of the world, toward our last destination, which is the heavenly fatherland. We are only passing through here below. For this reason, nothing can give us as profound a sense of the meaning of our earthly life and stimulate us to live it as a brief experimental stage — and one of enrichment as well — as can an inner *attitude of seeing ourselves as pilgrims.*

Marian shrines are scattered throughout the world. They are like so many milestones, set up to mark the stages of our itinerary on earth: they enable us to pause for a rest, to restore ourselves from the journey, to regain joy and security on the way, together with strength to go on. They are like oases in the desert, formed to provide water and shade.

Insegnamenti, March 19, 1982

The Second Vatican Council, by presenting Mary in the mystery of Christ, also finds the path to a deeper understanding of the mystery of the Church. Mary, as the Mother of Christ, *is in a particular way united with the Church,* "which the Lord established as his own body." It is significant that the conciliar text places this truth about the Church as the Body of Christ (according to the teaching of the Pauline

Letters) in close proximity to the truth that the Son of God "through the power of the Holy Spirit was born of the Virgin Mary." The reality of the Incarnation finds a sort of extension *in the mystery of the Church — the Body of Christ.* And one cannot think about the reality of the Incarnation without referring to Mary, the Mother of the Incarnate Word.

In these reflections, however, I wish to consider primarily that "pilgrimage of faith" in which "the Blessed Virgin advanced," faithfully preserving her union with Christ. In this way the *"twofold bond"* which unites the Mother of God *with Christ and with the Church* takes on historical significance. Nor is it just a question of the Virgin Mother's life-story, of her personal journey of faith, and "the better part" which is hers in the mystery of salvation; it is also a question of the history of the whole People of God, *of all those who take part* in the same *"pilgrimage of faith."*

Redemptoris Mater, 5

Today, as on this pilgrimage of faith we draw near to the end of the second Christian millennium, the Church, through the teaching of the Second Vatican Council, calls our attention to her vision of herself, as the "one People of God . . . among all the nations of the earth." And she reminds us of that truth according to which all the faithful, though "scattered throughout the world, are in communion with each other in the Holy Spirit." We can therefore say that in this union the mystery of Pentecost is continually being accomplished. At the same time, the Lord's Apostles and disciples, in all the nations of the earth, "devote themselves to prayer together with Mary, the mother of Jesus" (Acts 1:14). As they constitute from generation to generation the "sign of the kingdom" which is not of this world, they are also aware that in the midst of this world they must gather around that King to whom the nations have been given in heritage (cf. Ps. 2:8), to whom the Father has given "the throne of David his father," so that he "will reign over the house of Jacob for ever, and of his kingdom there will be no end."

During this time of vigil, Mary through the faith which made her blessed, especially from the moment of the Annunciation, is present in the Church's mission, present in the Church's work of introducing into the world the kingdom of her Son.

Redemptoris Mater, 28

Gratitude, communion, and life: these are sentiments which unite us, pilgrims "gathered here in the same place," we who form the present generation of the Church, for whom

Pentecost has already occurred, gathered "with Mary, the Mother of Jesus," we wish to confirm our assiduity in respecting "the Apostles' teaching, fraternal union, the breaking of bread and prayer. . . ."

Insegnamenti, May 12, 1982

My dear brothers and sisters: as we celebrate the Marian Year in preparation for the third millennium of Christianity, let us join the Mother of God in her pilgrimage of faith. Let us learn the *virtue of compassion* from her whose heart was pierced with a sword at the foot of the cross. It is the virtue that prompted the Good Samaritan to stop beside the victim on the road, rather than to continue on or to cross over to the other side. Whether it be the case of the person next to us or of distant peoples and nations, we must be Good Samaritans to all those who suffer. We must be the compassionate "neighbor" of those in need, not only when it is emotionally rewarding or convenient, but also when it is demanding and inconvenient (cf. *Salvifici Doloris*, 28-30). Compassion is a virtue we cannot neglect in a world in which the human suffering of so many of our brothers and sisters is needlessly increased by oppression, deprivation, and underdevelopment — by poverty, hunger, and disease. Compassion is also called for in the face of the spiritual emptiness and aimlessness that people can often experience amid material prosperity and comfort in developed countries such as your own. Compassion is a virtue that brings healing to those who bestow it, not only in this present life but in eternity: "Blessed are they who show mercy, for mercy shall be theirs" (Mt. 5:7).

Homily, Los Angeles, September 15, 1987

You certainly know that I have cultivated the Christian practice of pilgrimage ever since my youth. On my apostolic journey as successor of Peter — from Mexico to Equatorial Guinea — visits to Marian shrines as a pilgrim have been some of the loftiest moments, from the personal point of view, of my encounters with the People of God spread over the earth, and with men and women, our brethren in the great human family. And it is always with emotion, the same emotion as on the first occasion, that I set in the hands of Mary most holy all the good that I may do and shall go on yet to do in service of Holy Church.

Insegnamenti, **May 12, 1982**

The Church, which even "amid trials and tribulations" does not cease repeating with

Mary the words of the *Magnificat*, is sustained by the power of God's truth, proclaimed on that occasion with such extraordinary simplicity. At the same time, *by means of this truth about God*, the Church *desires to shed light upon* the difficult and sometimes tangled paths of man's earthly existence. The Church's journey, therefore, near the end of the second Christian millennium, involves a renewed commitment to her mission. Following him who said of himself, "God has anointed me *to preach good news to the poor*" (cf. Lk. 4:18), the Church has sought from generation to generation and still seeks today to accomplish that same mission.

Redemptoris Mater, 37

The mystery of the union of the Mother with the Son and of the Son with the Mother on the Way of the Cross and the path of her funeral from the Chapel of the Dormition to the Tomb of our Lady; finally, the mystery of their union in glory, recalled by the little ways of the Assumption and the Coronation: The whole of this, well laid out in time and space and covered with the prayer of so many hearts, of so many generations, constitutes a unique living treasury of the faith, hope, and charity of the People of God in this land. Every time that I came here I was aware of drawing from that treasury. And I was always aware that the mysteries of Jesus and Mary on which we meditate while praying for the living and the dead are truly inscrutable. We keep coming back to them, and each time we encourage ourselves to return here again and again in order to immerse ourselves in them. In these mysteries is expressed a synthesis of all that is part of our "little ways" of daily life. All of this was assumed by the Son of God, and through his Mother it is restored to man again.

"To All the Priests of the Church," 11

Distinguished ladies and gentlemen in the brilliant perspective which the word of God opens to the eyes of faith, I express to each of you a warm invitation to persevere in your dedication to the noble cause of helping the handicapped. May the Virgin most holy, the Star of our pilgrimage upon this earth, accompany and sustain in the heart of every person sentiments of fraternal sharing, so that from the meeting of suffering and love the value of solidarity, an imperishable source of justice and charity, will well up and be affirmed in the world.

Address, Rome, November 21, 1993

May the Virgin Mary, always honored in your sanctuaries which are dedicated to her, make your important pastoral work bear fruit, and may she help all pilgrims to enter the will of the Lord more! And I myself, in the very dear memory of the many pilgrimages I have had the privilege of carrying out or guiding, give you my affectionate blessing.

Address, Rome, January 22, 1981

In the expression "Blessed is she who believed," we can therefore rightly find *a kind of "key"* which unlocks for us the innermost reality of Mary, whom the angel hailed as "full of grace." If as "full of grace" she has been eternally present in the mystery of Christ, through faith she became a sharer in that mystery in every extension of her earthly journey. She "advanced in her pilgrimage of faith" and at the same time, in a discreet yet direct and effective way, she made present to humanity *the mystery of Christ.* And she still continues to do so. Through the mystery of Christ, she too is present within mankind. Thus through the mystery of the Son the mystery of the Mother is also made clear.

Redemptoris Mater, **19**

17 / Virgin of Virgins

May the most holy Virgin, Mother of the Church, whose birth we celebrate today, that is, the radiant and promising dawn of the great work of man's redemption, help you in your reflection, open your hearts to a genuine giving, and lend you the courage to take on with trust and gladness the fruitful responsibility of serving the Church.

May my affectionate blessing accompany you always.

Address, Frascati, Italy, September 8, 1980

She [Mary] it was whom Paul VI presented as the Virgin who listens, the Virgin who prays, the Virgin who begets Christ and offers him for the salvation of the world. May she be your guide along the sometimes difficult but always exhilarating path toward the ideal of complete union with Christ.

Address, Manila, February 17, 1981

At Cana in Galilee, where Jesus was invited to
a marriage banquet, his Mother, also present,
said to the servants: "Do whatever he tells you"
(Jn. 2:5). Now that we have begun our
celebration of the Year of the Family, Mary says
the same words to us. What Christ tells us, in
this particular moment in history, constitutes
a forceful call to a great prayer with families
and for families. The Virgin Mother invites us
to unite ourselves through this prayer to the
sentiments of her Son, who loves each and
every family. He expressed this love at the very
beginning of his mission as Redeemer, with his
sanctifying presence at Cana in Galilee, a
presence which still continues.

Letter to Families, February 22, 1994

Mary is definitively *introduced into the mystery
of Christ through* this event: *the Annunciation*
by the angel. This takes place at Nazareth,
within the concrete circumstances of the
history of Israel, the people which first received
God's promises. The divine messenger says to
the Virgin: "Hail, full of grace, the Lord is with
you" (Lk. 1:28). Mary "was greatly troubled at
the saying, and considered in her mind what
sort of greeting this might be" (Lk. 1:29): What

could those extraordinary words mean, and in particular the expression "full of grace" (*kecharitomene*)?

If we wish to meditate together with Mary on these words, and especially on the expression "full of grace," we can find a significant echo in the very passage from the Letter to the Ephesians quoted above [Eph. 1:4-7]. And if after the announcement of the heavenly messenger the Virgin of Nazareth is also called "blessed among women" (cf. Lk. 1:42), it is because of that blessing with which "God the Father" has filled us "in the heavenly places, in Christ." It is a *spiritual blessing* which is meant for all people and which bears in itself fullness and universality ("every blessing"). It flows from that love which, in the Holy Spirit, unites the consubstantial Son to the Father. At the same time, it is a blessing poured out through Jesus Christ upon human history until the end: upon all people.

Redemptoris Mater, 8

St. Ambrose draws for us the portrait of our Lady, with extraordinary and realistic delicacy, as follows: "She was a virgin not only in body, but also in soul; completely lacking in any deceitfulness that stains the sincerity of the spirit; humble in heart; serious in speech; prudent in thought; sparing in words. . . . She put her hope, not in the uncertainty of riches, but in the poor man's prayer. She was always hard-working, reserved in talk, accustomed to seek God . . . as judge of her conscience. She did not offend anyone; she loved everyone; . . . she shunned ostentation, followed reason, loved virtue. . . . This is the image of virginity. So perfect was Mary, that her life alone is a rule for everyone" (*De Virginibus*, II, 2, 6-7: PL 16, pp. 208-210).

Address, Turin, April 13, 1980

At the beginning of the New Covenant, which is to be eternal and irrevocable, there is a woman: the Virgin of Nazareth. It is a *sign* that points to the fact that "in Jesus Christ" *"there is neither male nor female"* (Gal. 3:28). In Christ the mutual opposition between man and woman — which is the inheritance of original sin — is essentially overcome. "For you are all *one* in Jesus Christ," St. Paul will write.

Mulieris Dignitatem, 11

It is the Virgin Mary who invites us to consider history as an adventure of love in which God keeps his promises and triumphs with his fidelity. A history in which God asks us, as he asked the Virgin, to be his associates, his collaborators, in order to carry out his plan of salvation from generation to generation. This requires that we respond to God, like Mary, with a total and irrevocable *"fiat."*

Address, Caracas, January 27, 1985

The whole of Christ's life, from the beginning, was a discreet but clear separation from what so deeply determined the meaning of the body in the Old Testament. Almost in contradiction of all the expectations of the Old Testament tradition, Christ was born of Mary. She said clearly of herself at the moment of the Annunciation: "How can this be, since I do not know man?" That is, she professed her virginity.

And Mary's motherhood is virginal, even though Jesus was born of her as every other human being, like a son from his mother, even though this coming of his into the world was accompanied by the presence of a man who was the spouse of Mary and, in the eyes of the law and men, her husband. To this virginal motherhood of Mary corresponds the virginal mystery of Joseph, who followed the voice from on high, and did not hesitate to take Mary because "it is by the Holy Spirit that she has conceived this child." So the virginal conception and the birth to the world of Jesus were concealed from men. In the eyes of his fellow townsmen at Nazareth he was regarded as "the son of the carpenter" (*"ut putabatur filius Joseph"*) — as he was thought, the son of Joseph.

In spite of all that, the reality and essential truth of his conception and birth depart in themselves from what in the Old Testament was exclusively in favor of matrimony and rendered what actually happened incomprehensible and socially disfavored.

Insegnamenti, March 24, 1982

According to Jewish custom, marriage took place in two stages: first, the legal, or true, marriage was celebrated, and then, only after a certain period of time, the husband brought the wife into his own house. Thus, before he lived with Mary, Joseph was already her "husband." *Mary, however, preserved her deep desire to give herself exclusively to God.* One may well ask how this desire of Mary's could be reconciled with a "wedding." The answer can only come from the saving events as they unfold, from the special action of God himself. From the moment of the Annunciation, Mary knew that *she was to fulfill her virginal desire* to give herself exclusively and fully to God precisely *by becoming the Mother of God's Son.* Becoming a Mother by the power of the Holy Spirit was the form taken by her gift of self: a form which God himself expected of the Virgin Mary, who was "betrothed" to Joseph. Mary uttered her *"fiat."* The fact that Mary was "betrothed" to Joseph was *part of the very plan of God.* This is pointed out by Luke and especially by Matthew. The words spoken to Joseph are very significant: "Do not fear to take Mary *your wife,* for that which has been conceived in her is of the Holy Spirit" (Mt. 1:20). These words explain the mystery of Joseph's wife: in her motherhood Mary is a virgin. In her, "the Son of the Most High" assumed a human body and became "the Son of Man."

Redemptoris Custos, 18

Let us look to Mary: *Virgo paritura* (the Virgin about to give birth). Let us, the Church, . . . look, and let us try to understand better what responsibility Christmas brings with it toward every man who is to be born on earth. For the present we will stop at this point and interrupt these considerations: we will certainly have to return to them again, and not just once.

Audience, Rome, January 3, 1979

May you be assisted . . . by the Blessed Virgin! She, whom my predecessor Paul VI of venerable memory indicated in his Apostolic Exhortation *Marialis Cultus* as the Virgin listening, the Virgin in prayer, the Virgin who begets Christ and offers him for the salvation of the world, remains the unsurpassable model of every consecrated life. May it be she who acts as your guide in the laborious but fascinating ascent toward the ideal of full assimilation with Christ the Lord.

Address, Rome, November 24, 1979

For the kingdom, it is worth living this precious value of Christianity, priestly celibacy, the centuries-old heritage of the Church; it is worth living it in a responsible way, although it calls for a good many sacrifices. Cultivate devotion to Mary, the Virgin Mother of the Son of God, so that she may help you and urge you to carry it out fully!

Address, Guadalajara, January 30, 1979

Always and everywhere, Christian sanctuaries have been, or have been intended to be, signs of God, of his entrance into human history. Each of them is a memorial of the mystery of the Incarnation and of Redemption. Did not your poet Péguy say, in his original style, that the Incarnation is the only interesting story that has ever happened? It is the history of God's love for every man and for the whole of mankind (cf. *Redemptor Hominis*, 13). And if numerous Romanesque, Gothic, or modern sanctuaries have been dedicated to our Lady, it is because the humble Virgin of Nazareth gave birth, through the action of the Holy Spirit, to the Son of God himself, the universal Savior, and because her role is always to present Christ "rich in mercy" to the generations that succeed one another.

Address, Rome, January 22, 1981

The reading of the Gospel according to St. Matthew invites us to meditate on a particular moment in the life of Joseph of Nazareth, a moment full of divine content and at the same time of profound human truth. We read: "Now the birth of Jesus Christ took place in this way. When his mother Mary had been betrothed to Joseph, before they came together she was found to be with child of the Holy Spirit" (Mt. 1:18). When we listen to these words, there come to mind those other well-known words which we recite daily in the morning, noon, and evening prayer: "The angel of the Lord declared unto Mary, and she conceived of the Holy Spirit."

Through the Holy Spirit, the Son of God was conceived in order to become a man, the

Son of Mary. This was the mystery of the Virgin, who replied to the words of the Annunciation: "Behold, I am the handmaid of the Lord; let it be done to me according to your word" (Lk. 1:38).

And so it happened: "The Word became flesh and dwelt among us" (Jn. 1:14). And above all he came to dwell in the womb of the Virgin who — remaining a virgin — became a mother: "She was found to be with child of the Holy Spirit" (Mt. 1:18).

Address, Terni, Italy, March 19, 1981